"Anyone who works with faculty—Division Directors, Academic Deans, and espe[...] invaluable book close at hand. Independent School Management translates mis[...] reading *Comprehensive Faculty Development,* you will want to jump into creati[...] for growth. Refreshing and eminently doable!"

— Sarah Cooper, Dean of Studies, Flintridge Preparatory School (CA)

"I wish I had more years left in my career to guide others with *CFD* and help them see the results. This road map to continuous improvements is truly a gift to the profession."

— Daniel McDonough, Headmaster, Portsmouth Abbey School (RI)

"This is the book I've been waiting for. It pulls together and clearly articulates all of the aspects of bringing new faculty into the community and ensuring their ongoing success. This mission-based, student-centered framework is supported by ISM's trademark, rigorous research and communicated in a practical, accessible manner."

— Sheri Homany, Associate Head of School, Hathaway Brown School (OH)

"*Comprehensive Faculty Development* provides practical guidance and model policies for independent school leaders to implement tomorrow in their school communities. Thank you for outlining how to develop mission-driven faculty development procedures from the hiring to termination process while providing realistic scenarios that all administrators face."

— Adrienne Fourgette, High School Principal, Nardin Academy (NY)

"Our primary role as school leaders is to facilitate an environment where students are academically challenged and engaged by inspiring teachers. *Comprehensive Faculty Development* outlines in detail a plan that enables leaders to put all the elements in place to achieve that primary aim. Its step-by-step and easy-to-follow format also ensures that no one should have any hesitancy in adopting its principles. The book is a must read for any school leader and should be required reading for all who have the enviable task of leading a group of faculty members."

— Nathan Washer, Assistant Head of School, The Pine School (FL)

"*Comprehensive Faculty Development* provides a well-developed and thoughtful approach to faculty development. By separating the growth and evaluation components found in traditional faculty development programs, teachers feel free to learn and grow, and are more willing to take risks in the classroom. Student experiences are enriched and teacher morale improves when teachers feel supported to try new approaches."

— Jo Stoltz, Academic Dean, Episcopal Collegiate School (AR)

"I found the book delivers on the promise of its title. From a review of research of current teacher evaluation systems to orienting toward a new, more mission-focused system, the staff at ISM did a remarkable job in outlining not only an appropriate process, but, and more importantly, focused specifically on the 'why behind the what.' Having led the faculty evaluation process at schools for over 15 years now, I am more excited about the future of building capacity in my faculty having reviewed this book. Bravo to ISM and thank you for such an important contribution to increasing student performance, satisfaction, and enthusiasm for learning."

— John H. Suitor III, Head of School, Boulder Country Day School (CO)

"This book offers a well-informed look at how traditional, top-down evaluation actually thwarts teacher growth. Independently operated public charter schools are ideally positioned to build a different school culture—one that values teachers as professionals who are intrinsically motivated to direct their own growth while forming trusting relationships with colleagues who are empowered to support them. *CFD's* growth and renewal paradigm keeps teachers inspired, and it also addresses that 'hard-to-crack nut' of relatively flat organizational structures in schools where teacher leadership opportunities are scarce. Charter school communities will find this approach congruent with their missions, which often include site-based management, shared decision-making, and authentic 'ownership' of the education process—a 'win-win' with both teacher and, ultimately, student performance being maximized."

— Gregory Meece, School Director, Newark Charter School (DE)

Comprehensive Faculty Development
A Growth and Evaluation Framework for Teachers
Second Edition

Independent School Management, Inc.
1316 N. Union Street, Wilmington, DE 19806

Based on research and concepts developed by Independent School Management Consultants, past and present. Special thanks to Barbara Beachley, Madeleine Ortman, and Bryan Smyth for their significant contributions to this book. Edited by Weldon Burge.

Disclaimer: Independent School Management provides management consulting and other services to private schools. ISM is not a law firm. No service or information provided by ISM should be construed as legal advice. All references in this book are correct as of the publication date, but may have become inactive or otherwise modified since that time.

Printed in the United States of America

ISBN-13: 978-1-883627-23-2

Contents

Research Background, Evolution, and What Is Needed Now

ISM developed this book to guide private schools in answering this question:

How do we ensure that we have a great faculty that delivers the mission with excellence and ultimately increases student performance, satisfaction, and enthusiasm?

By supporting teachers, the school supports students and helps ensure the institution's long-term growth and success. So this book is not about *teachers*— it is really about *students*. We believe, by implementing the processes and procedures found here, the school *ultimately increases student performance, satisfaction, and enthusiasm.*

The Case for a New Model

According to research, "teacher effectiveness" is the dominant factor in student performance.[1] Given this, the education industry has long attempted to develop teacher evaluation systems to ensure that students have the most skilled and committed teachers. These systems have typically used a two-pronged approach:

1. use the results of the evaluation to drive teacher professional development, and

2. ensure that your school retains and rewards only the best teachers from year to year.

Despite the number of attempts and approaches, teacher evaluation systems have been maligned because of their failure to discriminate accurately between effective and ineffective teachers or drive professional development.[2] In other words, there is little evidence their use improves student outcomes. Put more boldly, *teacher evaluation does not work!*

Research findings suggest that this is primarily because of the structure of teacher evaluation systems and the culture that surrounds them—the process by which evaluators measure and judge a teacher's effectiveness. Typical evaluation processes contain factors that inhibit teacher development and student achievement. Research has found the following.

- School administrators often, for a multitude of reasons, do not make enough classroom observations to evaluate teacher performance accurately. The primary responsibility of academic administrators is to build the capacity of the faculty to deliver a high-quality education and allocate 25%–50% of their weekly time in service to faculty development. This includes having conversations with teachers to drive their development, doing research and developing themselves, taking notes, observing classes to watch for outcomes of development efforts, providing feedback, and writing formal periodic evaluations.

  However, most practitioners don't come close to meeting this goal, and many protest that it would be impossible to do so with the other duties on their plates. Research has found they spend about 5% of their time preparing for or conducting classroom observations, providing instructive feedback, and formally evaluating teachers, and less than 1% coaching teachers to improve instruction and teaching. This raises serious questions about the ability of the process to result in meaningful and sufficient knowledge of teachers' work. It also gives rise to the serious issue of coaching credibility. How valuable are evaluations and coaching for development if teachers believe the evaluator does not "know them" as a teacher?

- There is little variance among teachers on performance measures. In theory, evaluation systems should measure and identify each teacher's strengths and weaknesses with reliability and validity. It was noted in *The Widget Effect,*[3] a large-scale report on the state of teacher evaluation, that, in reality, teacher evaluation systems do not distinguish between good and poor teachers nor identify strengths or weaknesses. In fact, this research found the systems result in virtually no variation among teachers. Almost all teachers are rated "above average."

- Research further suggests that the desire to avoid interpersonal conflict influences this problem.[4] The systems do not result in real discernment and documentation of teacher quality. Yet being able to make this distinction is a prerequisite for achieving either of the two aims the systems are designed to accomplish (i.e., to drive professional development, and retain and reward the best teachers).

- Nearly three of four teachers report their last evaluation failed clearly to identify any developmental areas.[5] This is not surprising, as teachers are often evaluated on long, comprehensive lists of items. This is problematic because evaluators simply do not have a defensible basis on which to judge teachers along all aspects of the list. Since most teachers are rated as "above average" or "meets expectations," it also means it is next to impossible for teachers to have an identifiable area of development on which they can focus. The volume of "things I do well, but could get better at because I don't 'exceed expectations'" is simply overwhelming.

- There is a significant debate about the specific aspects of teacher performance that should be evaluated, and the list is ever-changing as research uncovers new directions and recommended practices for teaching and learning. For example, some teachers may currently be evaluated on "differentiation" (i.e., matching lessons to each student's learning style preference). However, more recent research has revealed that differentiation does not improve student performance.[6] When teachers are evaluated, and then seek to improve their teaching based on aspects that turn out to be unrelated to student performance, the system itself causes lack of progress.

- Regardless of the cause, poorly implemented teacher evaluation systems can drive the faculty to feel threatened or create a sense of unfairness that undermines the faculty culture. If the evaluation results are perceived as "high stakes," yet the time spent on the evaluation process and support for professional development is scant, then teachers will likely experience a significant lack of predictability and support in the relationship with their administration—which also impacts the faculty culture. ISM's research in private schools has found that a healthy, growth-focused faculty culture is a primary predictor of student performance, satisfaction, and enthusiasm, meaning unhealthy school cultures may serve to depress student achievement.

- ▪ Evaluation and growth initiatives have substantial difficulty coexisting. Used in combination, they have been found to undermine trust within school cultures.[7] Research suggests that external evaluative feedback inhibits the accurate self-assessment necessary for professional growth to occur.[8] Research has also demonstrated that under states of threat that produce negative effect, people resort to well-learned and over-rehearsed behavior patterns.[9] This can occur when people perceive a high-stakes consequence such as the potential for a contract to be withheld or an evaluation score to be tied to a salary increase. Negative effect promotes active avoidance.

  Extending this to the teaching realm, teachers who feel threatened by the nature of the evaluation process engage in behaviors that are in direct opposition to growth initiatives. Teachers may be less likely to take risks, try new ways of teaching, and learn new ways of doing things. This is evident when teachers are informed they are going to be observed. They are most likely to trot out a highly predictable lesson plan in which the teacher is the star—yet that is not the way they are expected to teach in today's active learning environments.

In sum, the existing faculty evaluation paradigms suffer from a lack of discernment among teachers, primarily because of a lack of administrative time spent in service to faculty growth and evaluation and a tendency to avoid interpersonal conflict. Further, there are serious questions about the validity of the specific elements administrators may assess. This leads to a lack of trust and a perceived threat, which undermine the chance teachers will honestly self-evaluate and actively seek to engage in growth.

Characteristics of a Successful Growth and Evaluation Framework

The real role of leadership in education ... is not command and control. The real role of leadership is climate control, creating a climate of possibility. And if you do that, people will rise to it and achieve things that you completely did not anticipate and couldn't have expected.

– Sir Ken Robinson

Through more than 40 years of ISM research and our own collective experience and observations, we believe the following.

- A growth-focused and healthy faculty culture is positively correlated to student performance, satisfaction, enthusiasm, and ultimately re-enrollment.

- Teachers must be ever-engaged in growth experiences.

- Teachers learn more from regular engagement and purposeful conversations with their colleagues than they do from conferences and outside presenters.

- Teachers' eagerness to grow, and a belief in their capacity to do so, are necessary to empower them to learn, try new things, and ultimately improve their craft.

- Professional growth is facilitated by the evaluator's ability to, in the eyes of faculty members, credibly and comprehensively enhance teachers' performance, support their growth, and provide a predictable evaluation experience.

- Evaluation by the school administration is inherently external and, if commingled with a "growth" agenda, undermines the intrinsic motivation and mindset of the teacher. Consistent with research, that approach also undermines the ability of the teacher to engage in the self-evaluation process.

- Evaluations, because they are always tied to real or implied consequences (e.g., size of raise, continued employment), represent a potential "threat" to those evaluated. This threat and its associated negative effect inhibit a person's ability to broaden his or her behavior patterns (which is what happens in professional growth). However, positive effect encourages exploration, flexibility, and acquisition of new behaviors.

- To the extent possible, schools must not let the growth and evaluation purposes become enmeshed. Growth and "high-stakes" evaluation are antithetical to each other. The former requires a positive and growth-focused mindset, while the latter often invites negative effect and the possible use of already-learned behaviors. Allowing these two concepts to remain enmeshed may stunt teachers' growth and leave student performance gains unrealized.

- Teachers' perceptions of the evaluation experience as predictable and supportive significantly influence the faculty culture and student experience.

- To comply with legal requirements, schools must evaluate teachers annually in a fashion that is accurate, realistic, and defensible.

Just as we expect teachers to continue to grow through research, experience, and feedback, ISM continues to learn, assess, and refine its processes. Our findings indicate a need for a process that:

- is based on the belief that the primary responsibility of academic administrators is to build the faculty's capacity to deliver the mission with excellence;

- hires and retains a faculty that models the mission and Characteristics of Professional Excellence;

- assures the best possible faculty through the hiring and induction process, fostering a culture that promotes and funds growth, provides competitive salaries and benefits, and supports mission-based selective retention;

- uncouples the growth and evaluation cycles;

- trusts in the faculty's professionalism. Unless a teacher has violated that trust, the evaluation results will not be the primary drivers of professional growth—that rests with the faculty member's own process of self-reflection and assessment;

- fosters a culture where classroom visits and observations by peer faculty members and administrators are commonplace, welcome, and guided by the teacher's, or the observer's, own professional goals—not a marginally applicable, generic list of "best practices";

- includes a periodic review process that addresses only the essential teacher expectations developed by the school. Essential expectations:

  – are easy to observe and measure;

  – constitute the necessary characteristics of professionalism in a school, rated on a dichotomous "meeting or not meeting" scale; and

  – have a breadth that is reasonable for administrators to assess every faculty member annually; and

  – have, as their only overlap between the growth and annual review cycles, the expectation that each faculty member is "authentically engaged in self-reflection and annual development of a growth and renewal plan." This includes developing written goals and making progress toward these goals. Engagement in designing and implementing improved teaching methods for oneself and one's colleagues is the norm. What that looks like is personalized to each teacher, driven by that teacher's own self-assessment, and supported by the coaching and collaborative relationship(s) the faculty has at the school.

Using This Book

The most important element of our Comprehensive Faculty Development model is the separation of the growth and evaluation cycles and the resultant change in how coaches engage in the "ongoing conversation" and use observations differently. Relatedly, the two sets of expected behaviors specific to each of the two cycles takes on paramount importance. The first is the Characteristics of Professional Excellence, a set of higher-order performance traits used as the basis for hiring, inducting, recognizing, and developing teachers to ensure a growth-oriented faculty culture. The second is defined as Essential Expectations, which are nonnegotiable and on which teachers are evaluated and selectively retained. They are the only components on which faculty members are formally evaluated.

The discrete sections in this book can stand on their own, but also link to one another. You need not read the book cover to cover like a novel. Get well-acquainted, however, with the general framework, important elements, and implementation of the process.

After reviewing this information, the reader is well-positioned to focus on the sections of main interest to him or her (e.g., hiring, evaluation, or compensation). Of course, we encourage you to work through the entire text to gain an in-depth sense of how all the processes fit together. If time is limited, however, focusing only on the section(s) of immediate interest (after absorbing the background information) still serves your needs well.

Legal Compliance

With regard to legal compliance, school leaders should be aware that educational institutions are bound by nearly all the same laws, statutes, and regulations that govern other private organizations. Administrators do not need to become legal experts. However, it is a necessary part of management to be aware of the employment and benefits laws with which the school must comply. To this end, we have included a legal overview as part of the book. Review the policies and procedures of this iteration of Comprehensive Faculty Development with the school's attorney to ensure requisite compliance and protections are attained in your jurisdiction.

Definitions

Throughout this book, we use various terms to represent private school administrators, including the School Head, Division Director, Manager, Supervisor, and Administrator. As titles and roles vary from school to school, for purposes of discussion in this book, we generally intend these terms to mean the following.

- **School Head:** The top administrator in your school—the person with the responsibility for the entire school operation, who is hired by and reports to the Board of Trustees. Various titles may include Headmaster or Headmistress, President, Superintendent, Executive Director, or Principal.

- **Division Director:** An administrator who oversees the operations of a division (e.g., lower school, middle school, upper school). Various titles may include Division Head, Principal, or Director.

- **Manager, Supervisor, or Academic Administrator:** Describes a function more than a level or a title. It describes any person responsible for managing teachers in a school. This may include the School Head, Division Directors, Department Chairs, Grade Coordinators, and Deans of Faculty.

Please note: It is important not to allow title references to distract from the content presented. That is to say, in most cases, we use titles for example purposes and not for prescriptive purposes. We don't intend to suggest who should carry out such-and-such task or hold such-and-such responsibility, other than the general prescription that an administrator with the proper authority, skill, and training should implement the suggested task.

Perspective and Encouragement

We have observed that many private school leaders have received outstanding training on *academic* matters, but often less (or no) training on *personnel-related* matters. This can result in administrators who are hesitant to embrace certain aspects of their managerial duties. We hope that reading this book is an empowering experience. Educate yourself about important employee-related principles that are most likely to lead to the greatest success for the students in your school.

Determining exactly what actions are necessary to bring these principles to life in your school may not always come easily (and rarely without deep reflection and assessment). However, by following the processes outlined in this book, you can be confident that you have done your best to achieve your school's standard of excellence this year and sustain it into the future. And you will have done so in the most mission-appropriate, legal, and effective manner.

An Important Note

The principles, processes, tools, and techniques outlined in this book focus on teacher-specific practices. The needs of the faculty and the vital strategic importance of faculty culture necessitate a model tuned directly to the teachers. Therefore, the model presented in this book is not intended for use for other roles in your organization. ISM has developed different (but aligned) processes for driving growth and conducting evaluations of the School Head, administrators, and nonteaching staff. Using the set of growth and evaluation systems together is recommended to strengthen the school across the board.

Source Material and ISM

This book is written based on ISM's experience since 1975 in guiding private school administrators. It reflects our current knowledge of research and strategies in the human resources, performance, evaluation, growth and renewal, management, and leadership fields of study. Key elements are derived from the ISM-led Research on School Management (RSM) and Student Experience Study (SES) research studies described in the "Purpose and Outcomes" chapter.

The book also draws together content from ISM articles, books, presentations, workshops, webinars, and podcasts published over the years that focus on attracting, retaining, developing, and inspiring faculty members.

---

[1] Wright, P., Horn, S.P. & Sanders, W.L. (1997). "Teacher and Classroom Context Effects on Student Achievement: Implications for Teacher Evaluation." Journal of Personnel Evaluation in Education 11: 57-67, 1997.

[2] Marzano, R.J. (2012). "The Two Purposes of Teacher Evaluation." Educational Leadership 70, 3. http://www.ascd.org/publications/educational-leadership/nov12/vol70/num03/The-Two-Purposes-of-Teacher-Evaluation.aspx

[3] Weisberg, D., Sexton, S., Mulhern, J. & Keeling, D. (2009). The Widget Effect: Our National Failure to Acknowledge and Act on Differences in Teacher Effectiveness. 2nd Edition.

[4] Grissom, J. A. and Loeb, S. (2017). "Assessing Principals' Assessments: Subjective Evaluations of Teacher Effectiveness in Low- and High-Stakes Environments." Education Finance and Policy 2017 12:3, 369-395.

[5] Horng, E. L., Klasik, D. and Loeb, S. (2009). "Principal time-use and school effectiveness." (School Leadership Research Report No. 09-3). Stanford, CA: Stanford University, Institute for Research on Education Policy & Practice.

[6] Willingham, D. (2009). Why Don't Students Like School?: A Cognitive Scientist Answers Questions About How the Mind Works and What it Means for the Classroom. San Francisco, CA: Jossey-Bass.

[7] Bryk, A.S. & Schneider, B. (2004). Trust in schools: A core resource for improvement. New York, NY: Russell Sage Foundation.

[8] Sanford, C. (1995). Myths of organizational effectiveness at work. Battle Ground, WA: Spring Hill Publications.

[9] Fredrickson, B.L., & Losada, M. F. (2005). Positive affect and the complex dynamics of human flourishing. American Psychologist, 60, 7, 678-686.

About ISM

Independent School Management (ISM) is a research entity, publisher, consulting firm, and risk management and insurance services provider—the only comprehensive management support firm for private schools. Founded in 1975 and based in Wilmington, DE, our privately held firm has helped guide thousands of schools in North America and throughout the world.

Administrators in private schools of all types and sizes turn to ISM for advice and assistance on an array of management challenges, including:

- student recruitment and retention,

- fundraising and development,

- strategic and long range planning,

- Board-Head relations,

- scheduling,

- business operations,

- leadership training, and

- risk management.

ISM Consultants monitor trends in education, carry out original research, and author the private school management advisory letter, *Ideas & Perspectives*. Besides conducting on-campus consultations for more than 100 schools annually, ISM's Consultants lead workshops for school personnel throughout the school year in various settings and at ISM's Summer Institute and Advancement Academy.

In addition, ISM makes available insurance and benefits programs (such as health benefits, liability insurance, student accident, and other student, employee, and director coverage) that are tailored specifically to private school needs.

While ISM research and consulting focuses primarily on private schools, the majority of the framework described in this book is relevant to public and charter schools, as well.

The Comprehensive Faculty Development Model: An Overview

This book's introduction began with a question: "How do we essure that we have a great faculty that delivers the mission with excellence and ultimately increases student performance, satisfaction, and enthusiasm?" ISM's Comprehensive Faculty Development (CFD) Framework, intended to visually represent the relationships among the various elements that answer that question, includes three components: Mission-Based Onboarding, Growth and Renewal, and Evaluation. Excellence in each component is essential for CFD to work optimally.

Figure 1.1

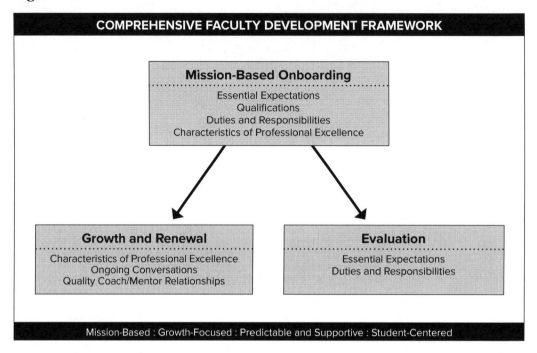

The Environment

The base of Figure 1.1, and all subsequent figures, includes four critical elements: Mission-Based, Growth-Focused, Predictable and Supportive, and Student-Centered. Schools successful in implementing CFD must nurture an environment grounded in each of these four elements.

1. **Mission-based:** The school knows and lives its mission. The mission provides focus and clear direction for all major decisions.

2. **Growth-focused:** Faculty professional growth and development is a cultural norm within the school. A growth-focused faculty culture underpins an inspiring workplace because of the opportunities teachers have to grow and renew throughout their careers. School leadership supports and provides resources in the form of time, expertise, and money for this growth.

3. **Predictable and supportive:** A culture of predictability and support is pervasive in the entire community, from the Board to School Head, School Head to management, Division Heads to the faculty, and teachers to the students. To perform optimally, teachers, just like students, need a predictable environment in which they are aware of what is expected

of them and how they will be evaluated. Faculty members also require a supportive environment where they receive the resources, encouragement, and guidance necessary to develop their skills for the benefit of students. Each teacher must also contribute to the predictable and supportive environment, modeling these principles in action toward students, colleagues, and managers. This can be assessed formally through ISM's Faculty Experience Survey (FES). (See Chapter Ten: Assessing the School's Faculty Culture and CFD Implementation.)

4. **Student-centered:** Students are the priority as decisions are made. Adults constantly and explicitly ask the reasons behind these decisions. The goal is to improve the learning experience for students and deliver on the promise implied by the school's Portrait of the Graduate (POG). (See Chapter Two.)

When it comes to driving improvements in student experience and performance, CFD will be severely hindered if it lacks any of these elements. As a result, schools must pay attention to these basic elements before engaging in a new plan. However, also recognize that successful implementation of CFD should enhance these four basic environmental aspects.

The Components

The Mission-Based Onboarding Process

The Mission-Based Onboarding Process (Figure 1.2) includes three components: mission-based hiring, orientation and induction, and mentoring. The goal of the onboarding process is to attract, hire, and support new teachers as they adjust to the school's social, cultural, and performance expectations. (See Chapters Three and Four for an in-depth discussion for each component.)

The Essential Expectations (EE), qualifications, duties and responsibilities, and Characteristics of Professional Excellence (CPE) are:

– communicated in the position description;

– used to inform interview questions; and

– considered carefully as a significant aspect of each hiring decision.

These elements also provide the basis of a thorough induction process.

Figure 1.2

MISSION-BASED ONBOARDING PROCESS

Mission-Based Hiring
Essential Expectations
Qualifications
Duties and Responsibilities
Characteristics of Professional Excellence

Orientation
Community-Building
and Preparation for the Start of the Year

Induction and Mentoring
(Teachers New to Profession and
Experienced Teachers New to School)
Ongoing conversations about mission
and values, pedagogy, culture & practice
over multiple years

Mission-Based : Growth-Focused : Predictability and Support : Student-Centered

The Growth and Renewal Cycle

The Growth and Renewal Cycle (Figure 1.3), outlined in Chapter Six, begins with the school's Characteristics of Professional Excellence as its foundational element. Both the faculty and the administration use the CPE as a guide to drive their development efforts.

Figure 1.3

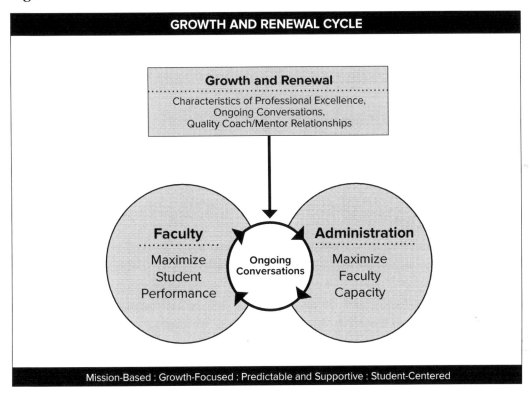

The Faculty's Central Purpose

ISM has found, in conversations with thousands of teachers across the nation, that too many fail to understand their true central purpose. When asked, "What do you do?" they respond, "I teach [insert subject here]." That is inaccurate as they don't teach mathematics, art, or English—they teach students. These teachers often believe their central purpose is to deliver their curriculum. This small error in perspective makes a big difference in the priority they place on professional development.

If their main purpose is to deliver curriculum (or prepping for an end-of-course test), then keeping up with the syllabus takes most of their time as they try to fit in as much curriculum as possible into, at most, 180 days. (Private schools typically have fewer than 180 published days of school.) Professional development is something you do when you finish planning and grading.

On the other hand, teachers who consider their purpose to teach children view covering the syllabus of tertiary importance; it is not how much a teacher covers but how much each student masters. So, they are constantly challenging their plans, assessments, and assignments as they contemplate how to use various pedagogical approaches to improve student outcomes. Clearly, these teachers see planning as a process synonymous with professional development. Planning requires understanding the impact of the current approach, developing ideas into what might work better, incorporating those ideas into lesson plans, and then re-evaluating.

With the student at the center, the teacher's question is: "How might I improve to better maximize student performance?" That outcome—maximizing student performance—is the essential purpose for every teacher. At any one moment, expect teachers to be making progress toward one or two written professional developmental goals. (See Chapter Seven.)

The Administration's Central Purpose

Similarly, administrators' primary focus is to maximize the capacity of the faculty to deliver on the school's Purpose and Outcome Statements. These statements consist of the school's mission, Characteristics of Professional Excellence, and Portrait of the Graduate (See Chapter Two). As referenced in the introduction, administrators spend less than 5% of their time each week in service to growth-and-evaluation-related tasks. However, ISM has found the student experience of the faculty culture is positively related to student performance and enrollment demand. With that, clearly guiding the health of the school culture and the quality of the faculty must be leadership's top priority. Spending the time necessary to develop and nurture culture, and engaging in their own development and well-being, would be a step forward in establishing a growth-focused faculty culture (one of the four environmental preconditions noted above).

The Ongoing Conversations

The mechanism by which the administration and faculty team up to fulfill their respective central purposes is the Ongoing Conversations. This term broadly refers to multiple robust, passionate, positive exchanges of ideas and information between the teacher and his or her coach or mentor. This supports the teacher in reaching the two professional goals he or she has articulated.

The conversations provide opportunity for:

- – the teacher to articulate and refine goals;
- – the coach and teacher to brainstorm ways to achieve individual developmental goals;
- – the teacher to communicate resource needs;
- – administrators to provide ideas and support, and to reinforce expectations; and
- – the teacher to demonstrate his or her engagement in the growth process— one of the Essential Expectations (see below).

These conversations take many forms, such as hallway chats, classroom observations and feedback, teachers dropping in to the administrator's open door, and emails or notes. They may also be regularly scheduled meetings. While some of these examples appear to be mere happenstance, this is not the intention. Teachers and administrators should look for opportunities to initiate conversational moments.

This ongoing exchange replaces the traditional model (the supervisor observes a classroom annually to evaluate and provide feedback to drive faculty growth and renewal). It's essential that the Ongoing Conversations are effective. They must be valued within the school culture, and the coaches and mentors must be committed and approachable.

The Evaluation Process

While CFD represents a shift to increased focus on growth and renewal and a reduced focus on evaluation, formal periodic reviews do serve to confirm that each teacher is performing at the requisite level of professionalism. In the event a teacher is not meeting expectations, it also provides a process for documented corrective action and, if necessary, legal documentation and protection, should nonrenewal or dismissal be required.

ISM'S Essential Expectations

Evaluations are based on a set of expectations that constitute the critical areas of performance. However, they are less about teaching and pedagogy and more about being a model employee, colleague, and professional. Listed below is ISM's sample version.

All teachers at Exempli Gratia Academy (a fictional K–12 private coed day school) are expected and required to:

- overtly support and act in accordance with the school's mission and values;

- foster a safe, predictable, and supportive environment for students;

- interact with colleagues in a respectful and collegial manner that fosters a healthy faculty culture;

- demonstrate appropriate planning and preparation for instruction;

- uphold professional standards of personal presentation, punctuality, professional courtesy, and discretion;

- appropriately carry out specific assignments, including but not limited to service learning, advisory programs, assigned supervision, and other areas as determined by the supervisor;

- maintain professional credentials, as appropriate;

- honor the confidentiality of school, student, and family information;

- comply with all school policies and procedures as articulated in the school's faculty handbook; and

- authentically engage in self-reflection and annual personal and professional growth. This includes written goals and progress toward those goals.

Schools may choose to adopt these items or modify the list to fit their needs (see Chapter Seven for guidelines). The one item that must be part of each list is the last shown here—engagement in a growth and renewal plan. This is the essential link between the growth and evaluation cycles. It allows leadership to judge whether teachers genuinely work toward improvement, but doesn't attempt to quantify the growth itself.

Armed with a set of Essential Expectations, evaluators must be visible in the community, collect relevant data (particularly when a rating of "not meeting expectations" is rendered), and nurture a predictable and supportive work environment. Conducting evaluations using the Essential Expectations is intended to be simple and easily accomplished through "management by walking around."

Figure 1.4

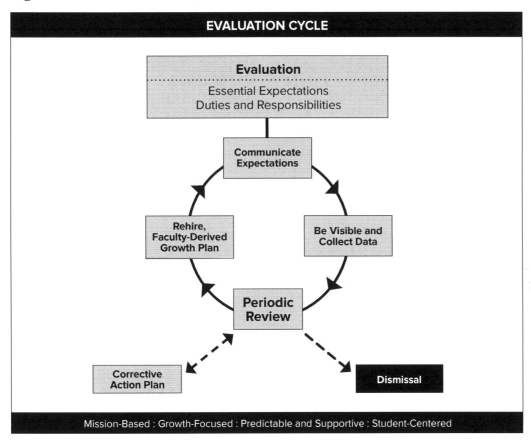

The Comprehensive Faculty Development framework assumes and makes it possible that all teachers are reviewed at least once annually at a meeting at which the evaluator formally communicates whether the teacher is performing his or her duties and meeting the Essential Expectations. Some schools refer to this as the "annual review." ISM has chosen the more generic "periodic review" to acknowledge that if an essential expectation is not being met, meetings will be held immediately to discuss the issue at hand in an effort to correct the behavior as soon as possible, and to allow for more frequent check-ins.

Referring to Figure 1.4, most teachers meet all Essential Expectations at a Periodic Review. When this occurs, the teacher continues the main path of the Evaluation Cycle, is rehired, and continues working on his or her professional goals in a self-directed fashion. If the teacher has not met Essential Expectations, he or she is either dismissed (for serious offenses) or formally placed in corrective action. (See Chapter Eight.)

If corrective action is introduced, the administrator prescribes the teacher's goals or expected outcomes. Depending on the nature of the issue, the supervisor may or may not direct the teacher to halt pursuit of the self-directed goals while working to improve performance. Regardless, a date by which corrections must be made and a time for a follow-up review are established. Failure to meet the expectations by the agreed-on date may lead to dismissal.

A final note: Neither the Essential-Expectation-based evaluation nor the growth and renewal framework form bases for merit-pay systems. Creating salary systems and setting criteria for qualification at levels or bands is a separate process. (See Chapter Nine.)

Summary

The ISM Comprehensive Faculty Development Framework is a three-part process including **mission-based onboarding, growth and renewal, and evaluation.** Schools that succeed in using CFD will be grounded in the four environmental preconditions for success.

Environments that are growth-focused, student-centered, predictable and supportive, and mission-based foster trust in the professionalism of the faculty and support a healthy faculty culture, which is essential in maximizing student performance, satisfaction, and enthusiasm. Supervisors can help to create these conditions and avoid the typical constraints formal evaluation places on the growth cycle by:

- becoming a skilled coach or mentor;
- allocating the necessary resources of time and money to professional development;
- setting and often communicating the school's expectations and purpose; and
- dealing fairly with those teachers who do not meet its expectations.

It is essential that schools empower teachers to grow and develop according to their own goals and professional interests. Throughout the rest of the chapters, this book takes deeper looks at each aspect of the framework and provides guidance on how to implement the full process.

Purpose and Outcome Statements

"He who has a why to live for can bear almost any how."
- Nietzsche

The Golden Circle: Starting With Why

If schools want their faculty to really engage in any growth and renewal process, they don't need compliant teachers. They need inspired teachers. How do you inspire faculty members—or anyone, for that matter—to action?

In his TED Talk "How Great Leaders Inspire Action," Simon Sinek, an ethnographer and author, partially answers this question.[1] He advanced his theory that there are three components involved in how an individual or organization can think, act, and communicate. Sinek organized these components into a visual of three concentric circles, which he called the "Golden Circle." A person's or company's "why" (i.e., a purpose, cause, or core belief) occupied the center, with the "how" (i.e., the process or approach) in the middle circle and the "what" (i.e., declaration of facts) in the outer circle.

His assertion is that most people or companies communicate from the outside in, beginning with "what" and "how" and often never getting to the "why." This is largely because we don't know our "why" and generally find the "what" and "how" clearer and easier to express. The resulting messages are flat and uninspiring and, most important, fail to inspire the action the company desires.

However, rare companies or people know their "why" and communicate from the inside out—from the "why" to the "how" and "what." Sinek's theory is that this approach is (1) more inspiring and effective, and (2) a significant component of their success. That is because communications made on an emotional level motivate and maximally influence decision-making.

Humans are not usually motivated to action by mundane facts or features. A description of a process fails to inspire us. We aren't intrinsically motivated for monetary gain. Rather, the idea that our work is important and means something motivates us. We are committed to organizations and people with whom we have a shared sense of purpose, and give maximal effort or make sacrifices for those with whom we connect emotionally. As op-ed columnist David Brooks wrote in *The New York Times*, "If you really want people to be tough, make them idealistic for some cause, make them tender for some other person, make them committed to some worldview that puts today's temporary pain in the context of a larger hope."[2]

Finding a compelling "why" can be a highly emotional experience. ISM regularly works with school leaders and faculties, helping them find their personal-professional "why" or core purpose. It is not uncommon for these individuals to well up with tears or feel suddenly empowered when making that connection. It's also not uncommon for people to avoid digging deeply into their emotions, as if doing so would be akin to jumping into the ocean, unsure if they can swim to shore. One school leader refused to engage, asking, "What if there is no 'why' in there?" Having a real emotional connection and finding a purpose is so important, blissful ignorance felt better to her than fighting through the fear of not finding one.

Due to the power of the "why," we agree that Sinek's phrase "start with why" has applicability in many school areas. Because the "why" tends to be less clear and harder to articulate and process, we often jump over it and go straight to the "how" and "what." A great example is when school leaders ask a question like, "Which is better—laptops or iPads? And how should we deploy them?" A good educational technology specialist can't answer this question without asking, "Why do you want technology at all?" Often we find that schools don't have an answer to that question. They have jumped to the "how" and "what" without clearly articulating the "why."

When a school decides to give iPads to all students without having carefully considered and clearly articulated the "why," it likely faces resistance from teachers and parents. Whereas when stakeholders are inspired by a compelling purpose, one they believe changes students' lives for the better, the response is far more positive.

Sinek approaches this topic from a corporate standpoint and has determined the appropriate order is why-how-what. However, in education, it appears the "what" comes before the "how." Consider the *Understanding by Design*® concept,[3] sometimes referred to as "backward" design. Calling it backward design is a perfect illustration of Sinek's point. *Understanding by Design* is really just a process for lesson and unit development that starts with the "why" (the essential questions), moves to the "what" (desired student outcomes), and last to the "how" (how to teach the lesson).

This is "backward" because traditionally we start with what we want to teach and how to teach it, often completely ignoring "why" we're teaching it. Although this book focuses on supporting and inspiring teachers, students are equally motivated by the "why," making it all the more important that everyone in the school community communicates from this perspective. Often we assume that everyone knows "why," including ourselves. It's important to stop and ask "why" at the beginning of every process, to make sure that we can answer the question in a compelling way. When it comes to articulating the "why" of CFD, we believe that when teachers are inspired to learn and grow, they pass that along to students, enhancing the student experience.

A note about Sinek's "Science": Sinek attaches biology and neuroscience to his theory, suggesting the "how" and "what" correspond with our prefrontal cortex, where our rational thought resides. He claims we make our decisions in the limbic system, which he believes is connected to the "why." As a result, tapping into the "why" or purpose or belief (i.e., thoughts intertwined with and partially driven by emotion) is a way to better inspire action.

Sinek's application of biology to his theory serves the goal for illustration purposes but is not fully scientifically accurate. However, the huge role emotions, including subconscious emotions, play in perception and certain types of decision-making are not in dispute. In fact, it is these emotional reactions to traditional evaluation processes, for the teacher and the evaluator, that subvert their effectiveness. Even if Sinek's scientific claims are overly simplistic, his codification has significant merit. When strong emotional connections, such as a core purpose or belief, are part of the decision-making process, an organization can tap into something strong and lasting for the follower or consumer.

Purpose and Outcome Statements

At the whole-school level, the three layers of the Golden Circle correspond perfectly with what ISM calls the Purpose and Outcome Statements (P&O Statements), which include:

- the **mission statement,** which communicates the "why" of the school (Why does the school exist? What is its core purpose?);

- the **Portrait of the Graduate** (POG), which communicates the "what" of the school (What specifically distinguishes the school's graduates from the graduates of any other school?); and

- the **Characteristics of Professional Excellence** (CPE), which communicate the "how" (How must our teachers approach their professions in such a way that the mission is delivered with excellence and the outcome is the Portrait of the Graduate?).

Most schools undoubtedly have a mission statement, and one or both of the other P&O statements. The question is whether the existing documents adequately provide the scope and guidance the school needs to define its purposes and outcomes in a directive, clear, and distinguished manner.

Mission

An ideal mission statement is powerful (gives goose bumps) and memorizable (no more than 12 words after the school name), guides decision-making, and rallies the community around a common purpose. The mission statement should accurately distinguish the school in such a way that current students, parents, teachers, and staff members recognize it as the school of which they are a part.

Applicant families and potential donors should have a reaction to the mission statement. It should attract them so they think to themselves, "That's a special place that I'd like to be a part of." Or, conversely, others say, "That doesn't sound like a good fit for my child or my values." Ideally there are more of the former, but if a mission statement is so generic to be neutral and appeal to all people, it won't be doing its job.

Consider the following mission statements.

- Exempli Gratia Academy nurtures children's creativity so they discover their own unique path.

- Exempli Gratia Academy vigorously challenges students to prepare them for success in a global economy.

- Exempli Gratia Academy supports young women to find their voice and capacity for leadership.

- Exempli Gratia Academy guides young men in strengthening and sharing their religious faith.

- Exempli Gratia Academy provides college preparatory academics in a nurturing atmosphere.

These five examples, while not meant to be exemplars, are clearly different and would appeal to different types of families, teaching candidates, and donors. A mission statement's primary function is to answer, accurately and powerfully, the essential question, "Why does our school exist?"

Too often mission statements answer the wrong question. For example, the last mission statement in the list answers, "What does our school offer?" It is far more a "what" than a "why" statement. If your mission fails to distinguish your school from your competitors, or is just too "soft," strengthen and clarify the statement.

Figure 2.1   **PURPOSE AND OUTCOMES**

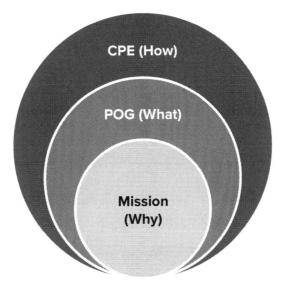

The mission statement articulates the "why" and should guide the school's decisions philosophically. But, without statements that address the "how" and "what," it is not definitive enough to provide guidance to the Board, administration, or the faculty in their pursuit of programmatic and teaching excellence. More is needed to communicate how the mission becomes visible in practice. In other words, *what* will it look like when it is delivered and *how* do you know you're able to deliver it? (See Figure 2.1.) The POG and CPE address these issues and round out your P&O statements.

Portrait of the Graduate

With a clear understanding of the purpose of the school's existence, the next step is to develop the Portrait of the Graduate. This portrait represents the "what," the desired student outcomes, and comprises three to five short descriptors of a student who has spent formative years as part of the school community. The portrait is the walking, talking example of the school's mission.

Consider these possible descriptors (these are examples only—each school's descriptors are unique). Students are:

- ready to perform with distinction at the next academic level;
- curious and committed to lifelong learning;
- intentional in examining the ethical implications of every action;
- competent in the use of technological research channels;
- eager to engage diverse communities;
- committed to community service principles; and
- able to model a lifelong wellness lifestyle.

Schools with explicitly religious missions may include explicitly religious descriptors in their portraits, such as:

- the ability to articulate fully the personal and ethical implications of a lifelong faith commitment; and
- being inclusive of, and conversant with, other religious viewpoints

The tendency is to be overly inclusive in POG statements, trying to make sure every aspect of the school's program is included among the statements. This is a mistake. Keep the Portrait of the Graduate concise, with no more than five statements. Do not try to string aspects together using commas to "hack" this five statement limit (e.g., an Exempli Gratia Academy graduate is "prepared to perform at the next academic level, workplace, and in life"). Even if "true," the statement's impact on readers diminishes as the list grows.

Once the Portrait of the Graduate is in place, revisit it during your quadrennial strategic planning events. The POG can be "tweaked" routinely without the kinds of ripple effects (through your community, your alumni, your accreditation agency, et. al.) that inevitably ensue with alterations to your mission statement. Use the Portrait to emphasize your school's uniqueness and continue to distinquish your school within its competitive marketplace.

For Comprehensive Faculty Development, the POG is an important source for helping teachers identify areas where they might modify their curriculum or pedagogical approach. For example, one of Exempli Gratia Academy's POG statements noted above is "competent in the use of technological research channels." Expect to teach this aspect not just in a required technology class, but in any class requiring research. If a teacher were not fluent in current technology research, he would determine that this was a professional development opportunity.

Characteristics of Professional Excellence

A school's faculty delivers the mission directly to the students. The Characteristics of Professional Excellence describe the qualities each teacher must display to deliver the school's mission with excellence and produce students who model the Portrait of the Graduate. The items relate to the mission statement and POG, but differ because they focus on the specific behaviors, values, and attitudes that must be present in strength within the faculty for the mission to come alive and the portrait to be realized. The CPE is the "how," inspired by the "why," that produces the "what."

The remaining portion of this chapter is dedicated to the Characteristics of Professional Excellence, not because this document is more important than the mission or the Portrait of the Graduate, but because these characteristics play a central role in the professional life of faculty members. Hire teachers based on the items in the CPE, which then serve as the primary source of inspiration for areas in which teachers choose to grow in their own professional development plans.

Development of the Characteristics of Professional Excellence

As with the Portrait of the Graduate, development of the CPE is a task initiated by the School Head. As a school embarks on this process, keep the following factors in mind.

Content

When creating the list, less is definitely more. However, it need not be as concise as the Portrait of the Graduate. A powerful, effective CPE:

- is a concise, action-packed list that vividly brings the key aspects of great teaching to life;
- focuses on items that are true difference-makers in students' lives and in developing and maintaining the faculty culture; and
- is short enough to be easily memorized and referenced regularly in the daily operation of the school.

Scope

The school should take a broad view of a teacher's responsibilities. Identify the characteristics needed in and out of the classroom when developing the list.

Teacher Involvement

Faculty participation is essential in creating the characteristics, since teachers define the essence of professionalism in each school, and this serves as inspiration for faculty reflection and growth. Without significant teacher involvement, the resulting list may be perceived as an imposition by the faculty. This can create defensiveness, preventing teachers from embracing the characteristics in a way that gives them meaning in the school's daily life.

The Process

1. The School Head selects a team to spearhead developing CPE items. ISM suggests that leadership create or identify a single group—not a group for each academic division—to compile this list. The CPE, once formulated, operationally defines what it means to be an exemplary professional faculty member in the school. Do not allow individual divisions to fragment this definition.

   Select team members that are bright, energetic, mission-exemplary, respected by their colleagues and their administrators, able to work effectively with adults, and excited about ongoing personal and professional growth. Some may be veteran teachers, while others are early in their careers. An ideal group comprises members who, when announced, are greeted by faculty members nodding, saying, "Of course, they are perfect for this task."

2. Give the design team a written charge, such as: "Develop a list of characteristics that vividly describe teaching excellence at our school and that are necessary to foster the characteristics described in the Portrait of the Graduate." Resist the temptation to elaborate on the charge other than to explain the overall purpose of the assignment, the intended use of the CPE, and the steps following this one.

   Show the group the examples above and encourage the group to conduct a simple internet search for examples from other schools as a source of inspiration. Many schools have created such lists. Unlike the Portrait of the Graduate, in which a short list of desired student outcomes springs to participants' minds immediately, this task may strike its participants as amorphous and potentially overwhelming. Sample CPE documents and the school's Portrait of the Graduate serve as a helpful departure point.

3. Usually, the School Head (and possibly Division Directors) meets with the team at least some of the time, particularly in the first session or two. This is when the group's charge is given and the members are in the early stages of sorting through and discussing the implications of the assignment. While it is vital that this be primarily a teacher-led project, it is equally vital that the administration not lose touch with the project to the point that it becomes disconnected from the ultimate results and fails to embrace and implement the outcome in meaningful ways. The dynamics of faculty-administration relations vary by school, of course. However, the administration must find a nonobtrusive way to stay in close and supportive touch with the project leaders while the team's work is ongoing.

4. Provide time constraints—preferably six to eight weeks. The quality of the team's product is paramount. It should not become a race to the finish because the group has run out of time. At the same time, a drawn-out process may inadvertently drain the passion and enthusiasm of team members. Whether and how to prompt a committee that is moving too slowly (or to slow down one that may be moving too urgently) is a matter of judgment.

5. When the committee delivers a completed draft, review the list jointly with the Academic Leadership Team (e.g., Division Directors) and the design team to ensure the characteristics:

   – are complementary with the school's mission, culture, and values;

   – reflect teaching excellence in your school;

   – are aspirational;

   – are appropriately informed by and infused with predictability and supportiveness; and

   – will be useful as guideposts throughout the Comprehensive Faculty Development Model (e.g., useful in hiring, induction, reflection, growth, and recognition of faculty members).

   If the document presented doesn't meet leadership's expectations, tread lightly here. Redirection calls for a well-crafted, thoughtful, and tactful response that guides the team carefully on this so the members don't lose heart or feel their efforts have been unappreciated. The teacher-administrator collaboration in the development process is meant to prevent this occurrence.

6. On acceptance of the draft, schedule a whole-faculty meeting and ask the committee to present its work. The School Head should provide the introduction, and then sit down while the members do the presentation. Suggest the group distribute copies of the completed list and, following the presentation, invite observations and suggestions for enhancements to be submitted electronically or by some other convenient written means.

7. Let the design team decide the next steps—let the team work until finished.

8. Unlike the school's mission, and like the Portrait of the Graduate, do not consider the CPE to be something that is immovable. While it should not be a moving target, changing substantially year-to-year, it can evolve. Since, as noted earlier, this serves as an important aspect of the hiring process and teacher growth initiatives, the list must conform to the school's current vision of faculty excellence within the context the school's other P&O statements, philosophy, and values.

Publication

When the final document is ready for public unveiling, schedule a whole-faculty meeting and ask the design team to present its work. It is the team members' time to shine—help them do so by accepting the finished product with appropriate expressions of private and public gratitude.

Use of the Characteristics of Professional Excellence List

Now the hard (and exciting) part begins. With the list of characteristics set, start using them in the daily life of the school. The three uses for this document are to:

– combine with your mission statement and Portrait of the Graduate to form a three-part foundation for all internal and external marketing efforts;

– serve as the basis for hiring and induction; and

– provide a common set of ideals around which faculty reflection and growth conversations are centered. See all the following chapters—starting with the hiring and induction process—for details.

Based on ISM's experience helping schools create their own list of characteristics, we offer a few additional reflections for consideration.

Skepticism

In schools where a culture of trust between the administration and the faculty doesn't exist, teachers may be skeptical about the project's purpose or utility.

This is especially true if their prior experience has been serving on committees whose work was put on a shelf and not implemented or accepted. If such a culture exists in a school, the School Head may wish to acknowledge the earned skepticism at the public kickoff of the project. Use effective collaboration with the design team and support their work to demonstrate a changing culture on an ongoing basis.

Jump-starting the process

If the team members are stumped on how to start getting the right characteristics on paper, they might consider thinking of their school's most exemplary faculty members. By identifying the characteristics displayed by these outstanding teachers, they may find they have put the heart of their list on paper quickly.

Creating an administratively driven list (not recommended)

Not all administrators choose to appoint committees to develop the school's list of characteristics. Some hold the view that their teachers are so overloaded with essential instructional responsibilities, or with some inescapable set of other responsibilities (e.g., such as preparing for an accreditation review), that this assignment would be a crushing burden for them. In these instances, the Leadership Team develops the initial characteristics, presenting a draft to the faculty for feedback before finalizing its work.

While this approach is highly efficient, its effectiveness is questionable. Faculty members may easily perceive the resulting document as something used to control (or, in extreme cases, even penalize) them, rather than something used to support and uplift them—spurring resentment and defensiveness rather than inspiration, growth, and renewal. Most Heads, realizing the implications, choose effectiveness over efficiency and find a way for the faculty to participate vigorously in developing the characteristics.

Refreshing the characteristics

As noted previously, do not regard the Characteristics of Professional Excellence as set in stone for the rest of the school's history. Examine it regularly—perhaps every fourth year or so—with an eye toward updating and further refinement. A renewed design team is the logical entity to spearhead that ongoing refinement.

Furthering the work of the design team

Once the team completes its work and the school has adopted its Characteristics of Professional Excellence, the committee may be disbanded. Use these developed characteristics in the school's next hiring cycle.

Characteristics of Professional Excellence
for Exempli Gratia Academy

For purposes of illustration, consider the following six-item Characteristics of Professional Excellence for Exempli Gratia Academy. This sample set of characteristics serves as the example carried through the remainder of the book.

Exempli Gratia Academy's Characteristics of Professional Excellence

The faculty of Exempli Gratia Academy commits to these characteristics as the foundation of our efforts to serve the needs of our students, colleagues, and school:

— models lifelong learning and the willingness to take risks that serve as growth opportunities, whether they result in success or failure;

— strives to live the school mission in word and deed, bringing it to life for students, families, and the school community;

— embraces and incorporates the most current technologies and media to support learning and prepare students for their future;

— fosters an open, inclusive learning environment that supports all students and their families through word, action, curriculum, and teaching strategies;

— enthusiastically engages in service to the school community and beyond; and

— maintains a healthy work-life balance and establishes expectations that ensure balance in the lives of students and their families.

---

[1] Sinek, S. (2009, September). *How Great Leaders Inspire Action*. Retrieved from Ted.com: https://www.ted.com/talks/simon_sinek_how_great_leaders_inspire_action

[2] https://www.nytimes.com/2016/08/30/opinion/making-modern-toughness.html

[3] Wiggins, G. & McTighe, J. (2005). *Understanding by Design*. Alexandria, VA: ASCD.

Mission-Based Onboarding: The Hiring Process

The goal of the mission-based onboarding process is to identify and select the right person for the right job in an effective and legal manner, and then integrate that employee into the school community. Breaking down the first part of this goal, and the focus of this chapter, note the following definitions.

- The right person is a candidate whose skills, characteristics, experience, and credentials are a strong fit with the needs of the position and with the school's mission, culture, values, and definition of professional excellence.

- The right job is a position in which responsibilities and required skills, experience, and characteristics are well-defined (for all involved on both sides of the hiring process) and well-designed to carry out the school's mission.

- An effective manner is a process that:
  - generates sufficient quality candidates;
  - respects the time commitments of the candidates and the school;
  - results in an objective, unbiased assessment of all candidates to make the right decision;
  - maintains communication and goodwill with the candidates throughout the process;
  - honors the dignity of all candidates, whether selected or not; and
  - reaches a selection decision with proper care and deliberation.
- A legal manner is a process that:
  - complies with the letter and the spirit of federal, state, and local regulations regarding antidiscrimination; and
  - minimizes the likelihood of the school experiencing (or losing) employment-related claims or litigation.

Addressing the second part of the goal—integrating employees into the organization—is the focus of orientation and induction processes. (Chapter Four details this.) The importance of these two processes cannot be overstated. The title and thrust of this book is about setting the table for all teachers to grow. Only with all parts of the model working together in a planned, integrated way will a school achieve its goal of regularly attracting and retaining energized, mission-appropriate teachers.

The Hiring Sequence

The following list represents the key steps in a Mission-Based Hiring Process (see Figure 3.1). We present them in short form to provide a sense of the flow of the process without interruption. Review each step in detail.

1. Review (or create, if necessary) Purpose and Outcome Statements.
2. Determine the Head's role in the hiring process.
3. Determine members of the recruiting team (aka "hiring committee").
4. Define the job requirements and performance characteristics and expectations.
5. Develop the marketing strategy for the open position.
6. Write and place recruitment advertising.
7. Receive and acknowledge candidate résumés.
8. Screen résumés against the established job requirements.

9. Select candidates for initial telephone screening interviews (optional).

10. Conduct remote (telephone or online video) screening (optional).

11. Select candidates for on-campus interviews.

12. Prepare for the interview—write questions in advance.

13. Conduct on-campus interviews.

14. Assess results of interviews.

15. Invite final candidate(s) for a guest teaching demonstration.

16. Check professional references and conduct background verification on finalist candidate(s).

17. Select the final candidate.

18. Determine the job offer.

19. Make a verbal job offer to the finalist.

20. On acceptance of an offer, issue the contract and notify nonselected candidates.

21. Receive the signed contract—set up personnel file and close recruiting file.

22. Launch the orientation and induction processes.

Figure 3.1   **MISSION-BASED HIRING PROCESS**

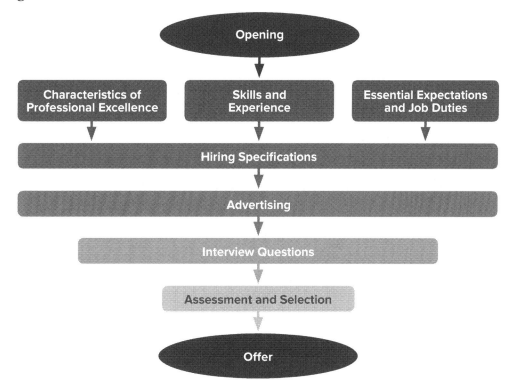

Step 1: Review Purpose and Outcome Statements

As noted in Chapter Two, the Characteristics of Professional Excellence (CPE)—one component of the Purpose and Outcome Statements—are not intended to be set in stone. They evolve as new programming, pedagogies, and philosophies are brought to bear on how the school delivers its mission. The likely annual hiring process is an excellent catalyst to initiate a review of the CPE, specifically each statement's continued applicability and effectiveness in serving as the bridge from the school's mission to its Portrait of the Graduate (POG). Enlist faculty leadership to comment on the CPE and take the opportunity in the prehiring process to adjust statements if necessary.

Some schools do not have a complete set of Purpose and Outcome Statements. When this occurs, the School Head should appoint a faculty committee (i.e., a design team) and charge it with developing a list of essential expectations and characteristics of excellence. Use these in all areas of school life involving teachers. (Review Chapter Two for instructions.) Develop this list well before beginning the hiring process so the list is not influenced by the pressure of "coming up with something"—i.e., when the need to hire is imminent and urgent.

As a practical matter, we understand that schools don't often have the benefit of operating under ideal conditions. Perhaps the School Head finds the hiring season is approaching and time does not permit the faculty committee-oriented process. Consider the following as a short-term alternative (after which embark on a full-fledged, faculty-involved process during the following term).

- **Phase One:** Identify Keywords and Phrases. Before the beginning of the hiring season, the School Head should meet with his or her academic administrators to discuss and reflect on the school's mission, culture, and values as they pertain to hiring teachers. Identify the keywords and phrases contained within the extant documents that may influence the skills, abilities, and knowledge of any new hire (e.g., mission statement, vision statement, list of values, taglines). Define what each keyword or phrase means. For example, if the mission includes the phrase "outstanding academics," identify words (three at most) that define what "outstanding" means. Then classify the words as either beliefs and reasons for this school's existence or desired outcomes and descriptors for future graduates (a proxy for a Portrait of the Graduate). Participants in Phase One should become well-versed in the school's mission and other documents before the first meeting. Then, that meeting should be of sufficient length to result in generation of the keywords and phrases, their definition, and the list of desired student outcomes. After a day or two for processing, the group should get back together to finalize a concise list of keywords and phrases that make up the proxy POG.

- **Phase Two:** Generate the draft CPE List. The purpose of Phase Two is to answer this prompt: "Develop for our school a list of characteristics that vividly describe teaching excellence here and that are necessary to foster the characteristics described in Phase One." The discussion should conclude only when each Leadership Team member has a firm and consistent view of what the school's mission, culture, and values look like in action and understands how these elements relate to hiring new teachers (i.e., the group shares a common vision of "what we are looking for" and why).

- **Phase Three:** Deploy for use in hiring. For practical purposes, these Leadership Team discussions need to result in a written list of well-defined characteristics pertinent to teacher expectations and excellence in the school. These characteristics and expectations must be communicated to—and absorbed by—all individuals participating in the hiring process (i.e., including the person responsible for drafting the job posting, all those involved in interviewing, and all those involved in planning for guest teaching demonstrations).

The most important element in the process is ensuring that all individuals involved have a common picture of what faculty characteristics are most important for success at the school. Once you define these characteristics and expectations, the hiring process can begin in earnest. Again, it cannot be underscored enough that this is a temporary version of the CPE items—the school must undergo the broader-based process outlined in Chapter Two.

Step 2: Determine the Head's role in the hiring process

The Head will want to clarify expectations as to his or her role in the process— e.g., the Head should:

- participate as an active and equal team member in all hires;
- serve as ultimate arbiter, deciding among the small group of finalists;
- meet with only the final candidate (selected by the committee) for formal approval purposes; or
- have some other role in the process.

Step 3: Determine members of the recruiting team

Depending on the Head's role and other factors—such as the size and composition of the Leadership Team and the number of job openings—the Head may designate a team to handle all faculty hiring for that season, or select a team for each opening. Make sure all persons involved in the process receive appropriate training concerning pertinent laws. All team members should have a clear understanding of their roles and responsibilities in the school's hiring process.

Step 4: Define the job requirements and performance qualifications

This is the most critical part of the entire employment process. The hiring team must ensure the essential skills, responsibilities, qualifications, and characteristics for the position are well-defined, as these elements are central to each remaining step of the process.

Use two tools to aid schools in defining job requirements: the Faculty Job Description Template and the Faculty Hiring Specifications Form. The use and purpose of each form is described below.

Faculty Job Description Template

The job description template is intended to help the school capture the primary responsibilities of the particular teaching position, including any physical, educational, or certification requirements. Avoid listing all possible tasks and focus on the three to five primary duties of the position. The key Essential Expectations must be reviewed as well.

Encourage hiring committees to select four to six Characteristics of Professional Excellence that have the most impact for the specific position. These characteristics help the hiring team distinguish which candidates are not only qualified for the position (based on education or experience) but also a match with the school's culture.

Note: All of the CPE should be communicated to each candidate, but it is often not possible (or advisable) to use the full list in every part of the hiring process. This is simply because of time and focus—i.e., the need to use every available minute of interviews to the best possible purpose. Ordinarily, a school's full list of Characteristics contain too many to discuss in one interview.

The following Faculty Job Description and Hiring Specifications Form (Example 3.1) is completed based on an opening for an upper school history teacher.

Example 3.1

Exempli Gratia Academy
Faculty Job Description and Hiring Specifications Form *(Example)*

Title and Reporting Relationship

Job Title: History Teacher

Employment Status: Full-Time, Exempt

Division or Dept.: Upper School

Reports To: Upper School Division Director

Supervisory Duties: No

Summary (1–2) sentences describing the main purpose of the position

Teaches a full load of history courses (anticipated 11th and 12th grade courses based on previous scheduling matrix). Serves as coach or assistant coach of athletic teams or moderator of clubs (or other cocurricular activities).

Key Responsibilities (List 3–5 key duties and responsibilities)

Responsibility 1: This position involves teaching a full load (four full credit courses) of upper school history courses.

Responsibility 2: For at least two seasons annually, serves as head or assistant coach, club or other cocurricular program sponsor.

Responsibility 3: He or she also serves as advisor to six to eight upper division students.

Responsibility 4: Authentically engages in self-reflection and annual development of a growth and renewal plan.

Responsibility 5: Adds in a positive way to the faculty culture, including being a trusted and supportive colleague, contributor to the professional development of others, and creating a predictable and supportive environment for students.

Other Responsibilities

Serves on at least one faculty committee during the academic year, as selected in coordination with the Division Head.

Minimum Requirements

Education: Bachelor's degree (required); Master's degree or higher (preferred)

Years of Experience: Six years of teaching history (required); at least two years of private school experience (preferred)

Specific Skills: Familiarity with classroom interactive display technology

Certifications: State teaching certificate (preferred); First aid (within 3 months of hire)

Characteristics of Professional Excellence

Select 3-6 from those below that are the most important on which to focus for this position.

- Models lifelong learning and the willingness to take risks that serve as growth opportunities, whether they result in success or failure.
- Strives to live the school mission in word and deed, bringing it to life for students, families, and the school community.
- Embraces and incorporates the most current technologies and media to support learning and to prepare students for their future.
- Fosters an open, inclusive learning environment that supports all students and their families through word, action, curriculum, and teaching strategies.
- Enthusiastically engages in service to the school community and beyond.
- Maintains a healthy work-life balance and establishes expectations that ensure balance in the lives of students and their families.

Approvals

Division Head _____   Date _____

Division Head _____   Date _____

Step 5: Develop the marketing strategy for the open position

Target advertising based on the position. Determine first whether to post the opening internally for consideration by current employees, and whether the search is local, regional, or national. Identify the best vehicles (or combination of vehicles) for that search, from the school's website to local publications to social media and educator recruiting firms.

Factors such as scarcity (demand and supply of candidates) and budget restraints play a considerable role. For example, for most faculty positions, a school may already have the benefit of a strong pool of local applicants eager to see which positions are posted each hiring season. In this case, a posting on the school website may more than suffice in generating a qualified, enthusiastic hiring pool. For harder-to-fill positions with exacting requirements (for example, an AP physics teacher with 10 years of experience), the school may need to consider a broader regional or national search.

Step 6: Write and place recruitment advertising

Employment ads should be consistent—in look, style, and tone—with the brand image the school promotes in all internal and external student and parent marketing and communication materials (Example 3.2). This serves several purposes—giving prospective candidates a much clearer sense of what the school stands for (and why they would want to work there), and furthering the school's image and message in the community. Irrespective of the medium, branding should be a central consideration.

Example 3.2

Exempli Gratia Academy
Advertising Example

Upper School History Teacher

Exempli Gratia Academy, a coeducational college preparatory school, seeks an experienced and dynamic educator to join its faculty as history teacher, coach, and advisor in our upper school. We enroll 400 students in three divisions (K–5, 6–8, and 9–12) and commonly place many of our graduates in Ivy League or other elite colleges and universities nationally. Our campus is located in the Anytown suburbs and consists of 40 acres of well-maintained buildings, athletic facilities, and a nature preserve. Our school motto, "Integrity, Service, Scholarship," describes our deep passion for preparing our students for future leadership roles in society.

In three or four sentences, "tell the story" of the school: key factors, overview of your mission, and why it is special to work there.

Duties and Responsibilities and Essential Expectations

This position involves teaching a full load of upper school history courses. In addition, we expect all faculty members to be fully engaged in the life and mission of the school, in and out of the classroom. The right candidate serves, for at least two seasons annually, as Head or Assistant Coach, club or other program sponsor. He or she also serves as advisor to six to eight upper division students. We expect a high-quality, experienced teacher for this role. All faculty members must also have an insatiable passion for self-improvement and a desire to join a community of colleagues who support one another in facilitating student success.

Briefly describe the job duties and expectations.

Education and Experience

Educational requirements include a bachelor's degree, with a master's preferred. Due to the strength of our academic program, we require teachers who have made deep, career-long commitments to teaching. In particular, this role requires a minimum of six years of teaching experience, with at least two years of experience teaching in the upper division of a private school.

State the educational and experience requirements or preferences (adapted from the Job Description and Hiring Specifications Form).

Skills and Characteristics

Teaching, advising, and personal skills and traits required for success in this position at our school include:

- use and knowledge of most current technology and ability to bring history to life in the upper school classroom;
- ability to foster an open, inclusive learning environment for all students and their families; and
- enthusiasm and dedication to contributing to our healthy, lifelong learning community, energetically supporting colleagues, sharing ideas and resources, and being there for others.

Identify the Characteristics of Professional Excellence (adapted from the Job Description and Hiring Specifications Form).

In summary, Exempli Gratia Academy is looking for a new member of our faculty community who loves upper division students and teaching history with a deep-seated, can't-be-contained enthusiasm, who will be energized by our collegial, collaborative, technologically advanced environment.

We encourage schools to include a summary statement that engages the reader and makes the school (and this position) stand out from other, more generic ads the candidate is reading.

We offer a competitive salary and top-flight benefits program, in addition to full relocation expenses.

Highlight key features of the compensation and benefits package.

Interested candidates should forward a cover letter, résumé, and three letters of reference by email to:

Eleanor Smith

Head, Exempli Gratia Academy

esmith@exempligratia.org

Application deadline: March 1, 20xx

Exempli Gratia Academy is an Equal Opportunity Employer.

Clearly state the application procedures and application deadline. If written references are required at this point in the school's application process, state it here.

If the school is actively seeking to foster a more diverse environment, it may elect to add, "We encourage applications from all qualified candidates, including those from diverse backgrounds."

This model represents a fully developed advertisement. It may not be feasible for a school to place this detailed an ad for all positions because of the expense. In cases where a more limited ad is necessary, the school may choose to:

– limit the ad to the school name, mission, and position title—and direct the candidates to the school's website (where the full position details can be posted); or, similarly,

– if the school has several positions open, list them and direct candidates to the website for further details.

The key issue is to make the full details of the opening (i.e., duties, skills, experience, mission) available in some manner. This prompts qualified candidates to apply because they have a good sense of what the school seeks (in terms of credentials and mission-related characteristics).

Step 7: Receive and acknowledge candidate résumés

Before résumés begin flowing in, the IT department should set up an automated reply. That way, when candidates submit résumés to the school's appropriate email address, they receive an automatic reply acknowledging receipt of the résumé and notifying them of how they will be informed of the next steps in the hiring process.

For example:

Thank you for your interest in our school. We have received your submission and will review your background against our needs for this position. We will contact you shortly should we decide to invite you to campus for an interview or if further information is required. We wish you the best in all your endeavors.

Step 8: Screen résumés against the established job requirements

The hiring team then begins reviewing all résumés received against the skills, experience, and characteristics requirements established in Step 4. The team may use any number of approaches to narrow the field of applicants, such as separating the résumés into three piles:

- candidates whose backgrounds closely fit with the position's requirements and will be considered;
- candidates who may be a fit, but whose credentials aren't as strong as those the in the top group; and
- candidates who do not meet the requirements.

Depending on the strength of the applicant pool—i.e., the number of qualified applicants for the position—the team may decide to extend the application period and place additional advertising to strengthen the potential candidate list before beginning the interview process.

Step 9: Select candidates for initial telephone screening interviews (optional)

Depending on the nature of the position and the number of viable candidates, it may be helpful to conduct an initial screening by telephone to whittle down a larger group to a more manageable pool of four to six semifinalists. If the hiring team can arrive at a workable group directly from the résumé screening process, proceed to Step 11.

Step 10: Conduct remote (telephone or online video) screening (optional)

The remote screening interview is a 20-minute conversation designed to:

- tell the candidates more about the position;
- gauge their interest level, salary requirements, and other expectations; and
- ask two or three questions about their background and skills to confirm they meet the position's general requirements.

The remote interview process ordinarily helps the hiring team focus on the candidates whose skills, interests, and expectations best fit the school's needs. For example, some candidates may decide to self-select out of the process after hearing more about the school's requirements. Or perhaps their salary expectations vary significantly from the range the school is considering.

Step 11: Select candidates for on-campus interviews

Candidates whose interests and requirements seem a match after the remote interview (or résumé screening) stage would then be invited for an on-campus interview. Send the candidates selected for on-campus interviews an agenda with the names and roles of those interviewing him or her, as well as information about any other expectations (e.g., teaching demonstration, lunch with students). Conversely, candidates who received a remote screening interview but who will not be invited for an on-campus interview must be notified they are no longer under consideration. Depending on the school's culture and the "touch factor" it wants to employ, make this contact by email, letter, or telephone. The loop must be closed in fairness to the candidates and so that the school maintains goodwill with them as a reflection of its professional, caring culture.

Step 12: Prepare for the interview—write questions in advance

For the school's legal protection, interview questions must be strictly job-related—i.e., based on the required skills, experience, and characteristics and expectations identified for the position. As a reminder, interviewers must avoid illegal questions about race, sex, national origin, and other non-job-related factors. (See Appendix A.) Many books have been written on the subject of interviewing. Consider the brief tips on developing and asking appropriate questions below. Provide hiring committee members and all others involved with more written and live training resources to further develop their interviewing skills and knowledge.

The hiring team should develop interview questions stemming from the candidate's résumé and employment application, and the Faculty Hiring Specifications Form. The résumé and application provide information about the candidate's job history, skills, and experience, which should be reviewed during a structured interview (see details below). The Faculty Hiring Specifications Form provides information about the school's required skills, experience, and characteristics and expectations for the position.

Behavior-based Interviewing

Behavior-based interviewing operates from the premise that past performance and behavior is the best predictor of future performance and behavior. That is, how someone has acted in past situations is the best (but not the only) indication of how he or she will act in future similar situations. Behavior-based interviewing emphasizes having candidates describe, in as much concrete detail as possible, the actions they took in previous situations similar to those they will encounter in their new school and in its classrooms.

For example, a typical behavior-based question in a teacher interview would be, "Tell me about a time when a parent reacted defensively in a conference with you about his or her child. How did you handle the situation, and what were the results?" Questions that begin with "Tell me about a time when …" will most often represent appropriate behavior-based questions.

In concert with behavior-based techniques, the interviewers should:

- ask open-ended rather than yes-no questions;

- take notes during the interview to recall specific examples the candidate described;

- prompt the candidate for more details with follow-up questions where appropriate (to give the interviewer a full picture of the situation or outcome being described);

- exercise discipline when asking questions. Allow time for the candidate to reflect on his or her answer before speaking (as opposed to the interviewer jumping into brief, awkward pauses and asking the next question prematurely, which often doesn't allow the candidate the opportunity to provide a thoughtful answer); and

- actively probe for contrary evidence—that is, if a candidate displays a strong tendency in one direction, probe if he or she also has tendencies in the opposite direction. This provides the interviewer with a more well-rounded view of the candidate. For example, a candidate's answers may demonstrate a repeated tendency to violate school rules. Instead of asking a follow-up question about other times the candidate violated school rules, the interviewer should ask a contrary question such as, "Tell me about a time when you followed school rules, even if you didn't agree with them."

Conducting a Structured Interview

For purposes of effectiveness and compliance, the hiring team should conduct the interview(s) in a methodical, planned manner. Working in a structured sequence of questions, the interviewers cover all the bases, from confirming the candidate's experience, to gaining a deeper understanding of his or her skills, to assessing how well the candidate fits with the school's mission, culture, and values.

As indicated on the following Interview Planning Form (Example 3.3), the interview should follow a logical sequence, as described below.

1. Welcome and rapport-building: Exchanging pleasantries; taking care of candidate's comfort (e.g., coffee, water, rest room break).

2. School's expectations for this position: Summarize the school's needs and expectations for this position, and for faculty members in general. (Note: A thorough interview generally lasts from 45 to 60 minutes. The interviewer should talk for less than 20% of the time, leaving 80% of the time for the candidate's responses.) Often candidates go through a series of interviews with various school constituents, including departmental faculty, academic administrators, and students.

3. School mission, culture, and values: Probe the candidate's understanding of—and alignment with—these areas.

4. Candidate's work history (résumé-based questions): The candidate briefly walks the interviewer through his or her résumé. Then the interviewer asks one or two clarifying questions as necessary (e.g., on résumé items that weren't clear or are particularly relevant to the school's needs in this position).

5. Required performance characteristics and expectations: The hiring team should develop one or two questions for each of the Characteristics of Professional Excellence and the Essential Expectations identified on the Faculty Job Description and Hiring Specifications Form (Example 3.1).

6. Candidate questions, status, and next steps: For purposes of goodwill and clarity, it is important to confirm with the candidate where the school is in the process and when he or she will be notified about next steps.

By using this structure, the hiring team protects the school by engaging in a consistent, job-related, nondiscriminatory process for all candidates. It also ensures the interviewing process covers the most important skills, experience, characteristics, and expectations relevant to the job. This gives the team the ability to make apples-to-apples comparisons of all candidates to help it arrive at an appropriate hiring decision regarding the candidate who most closely meets its requirements.

Tools

Record interview questions on a form such as the Interview Planning Form. This approach organizes the interview process, records a consistent set of questions (for legal documentation purposes), and helps search committee members know "who is going to ask what" of each candidate. It also provides a place for interviewers to take notes and summarize their feedback.

Example 3.3

Exempli Gratia Academy

Interview Planning Form (*Example*)

Note: One person from the hiring team can use this form to record the questions the team agrees will be asked of all candidates for the position. When completed, it can be copied or emailed to all team members, so they are operating from the same source when conducting interviews.

Candidate's name: Annette Richardson

Date: February 15, 20xx

Position to be filled: Upper School History Teacher

Interviewer's name and title: Kristen Grainger/History Chair

1. Introduction
   - Welcome, beverages, restrooms, etc.—making the candidate feel comfortable
   - Explain that the interviewer takes notes during the discussion and will ask the candidate to provide specific details regarding past work performance.

2. Brief Description of the School and Position
   - School's mission; key facts and brief history
   - Overview of main duties and expectations (e.g., teach five classes, coach two sports)

3. Mission-Related Questions (to assess how closely aligned candidate is with the mission)

Q1: Exempli Gratia Academy's motto is "Integrity, Service, Scholarship." Can you tell me a little about why you would want to teach in a school with this mission and how it resonates with your own goals and interests?

Q2: We strive to educate students to be "global citizens." What does this mean to you?

Candidate Responses:

R1: _____

_____

_____

R2: _____

_____

_____

4. Résumé-Based Questions (to confirm the candidate's job history, as indicated on his or her résumé)

Q1: I see from your résumé that your first teaching position was at XYZ School. Can you tell me about one or two of the most important things that you learned about teaching at XYZ that prepared for your next role?

Q2: Your résumé says that you "created and implemented a History Careers Speakers Series" while you were at XYZ School. Can you tell me about your role in organizing the series and what the impact was on students?

Candidate Responses:

R1: _____

_____

_____

R2: _____

_____

_____

5. Questions About Skills, Characteristics of Professional Excellence, and Essential Expectations

(Behavioral questions developed from the skills, characteristics of excellence and expectations selected as being the most important elements for success in this role at this school)

Q1: Professional growth is an important priority here. Can you tell me about the most important professional growth experience you've had thus far in your career? What brought it about? What impact did it have on you in the classroom?

Q2: When teaching, some students are easier to engage with than others. Can you tell me about a student who challenged your patience on a regular basis? How did you ensure that you supported his or her needs just as energetically as the needs of other students?

Q3: Can you tell me about a time you took a risk in the classroom and experienced failure? What did you learn?

Q4: Tell me about the most exciting lesson you've given or project you've led that applied "real life" experiences to the topic you were discussing in the classroom.

Q5: Can you tell me about the times you felt you were bringing the most and the least enthusiasm to the classroom? What affected your enthusiasm level? How did this impact the student learning experience?

Q6: Do you find yourself seeking out colleagues for joint projects or do you prefer to go it alone most times? Can you tell me about the joint project or collaboration that you're most proud of?

Candidate Responses:

R1: _____

_____

R2: _____

_____

R3: _____

_____

R4: _____

_____

R5: _____

_____

R6: _____

_____

6. Candidate Questions and Next Steps

- Ask the candidate what questions he or she has about the position and the school.
- Inform the candidate about next steps—e.g., another round of interviews, notification about his or her status.

Step 13: Conduct on-campus interviews

When candidates visit campus, they should complete two forms before interviewing:

- – Application for Employment and
- – Background Screening Consent Form.

Application for Employment

Schools sometimes shy away from using employment applications in their faculty hiring, feeling (or fearing) that prospective faculty members see it as unnecessarily "bureaucratic" and beneath their dignity as professionals. They believe— incorrectly—that it is "just the same as a résumé." However, applications provide protections for the school that résumés do not, making them an important part of a safe and effective hiring process. The application form offers numerous benefits.

- ▪ **Provides consistency:** One of the most serious legal risks for schools is an employment process that varies from applicant to applicant. By requiring all candidates to complete an application, the school ensures it collects consistent data—allowing it to compare applications on a fair and equal basis and avoiding inadvertent discrimination because of different treatment.

- ▪ **Communicates EEO commitment:** By including the school's Equal Employment Opportunity (EEO) statement on the application, the school is prominently communicating its commitment to EEO principles in the hiring process.

- ▪ **Identifies work eligibility:** Applications should ask the question "Can you, after employment, submit verification of your legal right to work in the United States (yes or no)?"—which forewarns the candidate that he or she needs to comply with the I-9 requirements if hired.

- ▪ **Identifies criminal history:** While almost no candidate indicates his or her criminal history on a résumé, the application requires disclosure of felony and misdemeanor convictions. This may provide information relevant for screening purposes and may disqualify the candidate from further consideration, even before running a background check. For example, if a candidate indicates a recent felony conviction for a violent crime or a crime against children, it is unlikely the school would wish to continue the interview process. (See the background screening section below for further details and guidance.)

- **Identifies reasons for leaving past jobs:** Few candidates indicate on their résumés reasons for leaving past positions. By requiring this on the application, the school can better understand the circumstances surrounding the candidate's career moves (e.g., whether he or she resigned to pursue greater responsibilities in a new school or was terminated or dismissed from a school).

- **Requires signing to verify accuracy:** All applications should include a statement in which the candidate vouches for the accuracy and completeness of all information contained on the application. With this statement, the school notifies the candidate that misrepresentations will be grounds for rejecting his or her application (or termination, if discovered after the person is hired).

As a matter of legal protection (to avoid discrimination or wrongful hiring claims) and good practice (being able to compare candidates based on the same data points), require candidates to complete an employment application.

Background Screening Consent Form

The school must comply with the Fair Credit Reporting Act (FCRA) regulations if it plans to order background screening reports (such as criminal history reports) from a vendor. To do so, it must have the candidate's written consent before it conducts any reference checks (including calling any professional references) or orders any background reports. To comply with FCRA, each candidate invited to the campus for an interview must complete a background screening consent form during the interview.

A background screening consent form typically requests the candidate's birthdate (commonly required by screening vendors to verify background information) and thus indicates the candidate's age. Therefore, this form must not be shared with anyone involved in the hiring decision to avoid age discrimination concerns under the Age Discrimination in Employment Act (ADEA). After completion, this form should be handled only by the person or office (usually the Business Office) responsible for ordering background reports on finalist candidates. It should be maintained in the recruiting file and should not be transferred to the candidate's personnel file when the person is hired.

States may have background screening notification provisions that exceed federal law. Schools should check with their background screening vendor to ensure the consent form they use complies with state requirements.

The Interview Setting

Conduct interviews in a quiet, private setting conducive to putting the candidate at ease and carrying out an effective interview. The interview should proceed according to the general outline indicated on the Interview Evaluation Form (Example 3.4).

Example 3.4

Exempli Gratia Academy
Interview Evaluation Form (*Example*)

Interviewer: Kristen Grainger

Candidate: Annette Richardson

A. Does the candidate appear to be a good fit with the mission, culture, and values of our school? Why or why not?

☑ Yes ☐ No ☐ Undetermined

COMMENTS

Annette spoke passionately about her commitment to developing "global citizens" in a way that aligns closely with our mission. She presented herself in a professional but friendly and engaging manner that is consistent with our culture.

B. Does the candidate appear to have the skills, be able to meet the school's Essential Expectations, and demonstrate the Characteristics of Professional Excellence required by the position? Why or why not?

Example: Skill/Characteristic/Expectation Demonstrated (Insert those from your school.)

1. Models Lifelong Learning ☑ Yes ☐ No ☐ Undetermined
2. Strives to live the school mission ☑ Yes ☐ No ☐ Undetermined
3. Embraces current technologies ☐ Yes ☐ No ☑ Undetermined
4. Fosters open, inclusive learning environment ☑ Yes ☐ No ☐ Undetermined
5. Enthusiasm for service ☑ Yes ☐ No ☐ Undetermined
6. Healthy learning community ☐ Yes ☐ No ☑ Undetermined

COMMENTS

The quality that stood out the most during the interview was Annette's passion for bringing "real-life examples" to the classroom. One example was her bringing a recently retired politician into class to discuss the legislative process. Of concern was her oversharing of her rehab history. While the history does not disqualify her, the possibility of boundary issues with students may be an issue.

Closing the Interview

In concluding the interview, the interviewer should:

- thank the candidate for his or her time;

- explain the next steps in the process and the anticipated time frames (i.e., whether the candidate will be interviewed by others that day, and the names and positions of those he or she will meet; at the conclusion of the day, the approximate date when the candidate can expect to hear from the school); and

- personally guide the candidate to the next interview or see him or her to the door if the process is complete for that day.

To wrap up our discussion of interviewing methods, we offer a vignette to bring several of the key points to life in a vibrant way (see "Sample Interview Dialogue" Example 3.5). Imagine the following scene:

Stephanie is an applicant for the English teacher position in Exempli Gratia Academy's middle school. On paper, Stephanie is the leading candidate, as her education, skills, and experience closely match the school's established requirements. Consider the interview that Robert, the School Head, conducts as part of the school's hiring process. What does he do right? What does he do wrong? Are any parts potentially illegal or discriminatory, or just ineffective?

Example 3.5

Sample Interview Dialogue
Note: We provide comments, observations, and recommendations regarding Robert's interview questions and techniques in the "commentary." You may wish to read the "dialogue" in full, then loop back to the commentary for notes and perspectives.

Robert (interviewer): Good morning, Stephanie. Thanks for coming in today.

Stephanie (candidate): My pleasure. It's great to be here.

Robert: Please have a seat. Is there anything I can get you—coffee, juice, water?

Stephanie: Water would be great. Thank you.

Robert: Did you have any problem with traffic this morning?

Stephanie: No. I'm a morning person. Ever since I finished rehab, I've disciplined myself to run at least two miles four times a week. So, I was up and out early—just as the sun came up.

Robert: That's great. What was the rehab for—knee surgery? ACL?

Stephanie: Oh, no—the other kind of rehab. I've had a few struggles with some issues in my life. I don't mind talking about it, if you'd like—it's part of the recovery process.

Even the most innocent question brings potentially controversial and discriminatory information in reply. Interviewers should be ready for this and prepared to deflect the question gracefully.

In this case, a simple question about the morning traffic leads to a disclosure of a past disability. The key issue is not to follow up with a question that is likely to prompt disclosure of potentially discriminatory information (such as any medical condition). This is an example of redirecting the interview to its core purpose without offending the candidate offering too much personal information.

Sometimes candidates just want to talk and share everything about their lives, even if the interviewer hasn't asked. In this case, the school must decide if Stephanie's candor and openness is a quality that aligns well with the school's mission, culture, and values—or if it is an example of poor judgment that may not reflect well on her ability to maintain appropriate boundaries.

Robert: [to himself] Oh, my. I didn't see that one coming. I probably don't want to go down that path. How can I get us back on track?

Robert: [out loud] I appreciate your candor, but that won't be necessary. (Pause). I see that you went to UM as an undergrad. Great school. I started work on my doctorate there. Beautiful campus.

Robert: [to himself] There—that wasn't too bad. This seems a lot safer ground.

Stephanie: It sure is a great school—what I remember of it, that is. You know—always a party going on somewhere. I could tell you some stories, believe me! But that was a long time ago in a different life, it seems. Anyway, it's funny how life goes—my oldest is considering colleges now and she's interested in their Junior Year Abroad program. She wants to study our family heritage firsthand.

Robert: What heritage is that?

Robert again prompts a dangerous line of questioning about national origin, which is a "protected class" under Title VII of the Civil Rights Act of 1964. It is safer if the candidate brings up discriminatory information than if the school actively seeks it out. That it comes up at all puts the school at risk. This heightens the need to have a structured interviewing process based on the job requirements. Establish a potential defense against lawsuits by asking all candidates the same questions during the interview process.

Robert: [to himself] Ooops! Should I have asked that? I'm just trying to make small talk. How bad could it be?

Stephanie: My father is from Eastern Europe and my mother is from Argentina. They met while studying in Mexico City during graduate school.

Robert: I see from your résumé that you're fluent in Spanish. Were you born in Mexico?

Stephanie: Actually, I was born in Costa Rica, where my parents were living at the time—we emigrated here when I was a year old. I hold dual citizenship.

Robert: Very interesting. That's terrific. Well, we've got a lot of ground to cover today, so what do you say we dive right in.

Stephanie: Sure thing. I'm an open book.

Robert: [to himself] She sure is an open book. I wonder if our parents would be happy with someone who is so "open" about her life. Hmmmmm. Anyway, we've made it this far—I guess I should just keep asking the questions and we'll see where we end up. I'm glad I wrote out the questions in advance or who knows what we might end up discussing.

Again, it is reasonable for Robert to wonder if Stephanie's candor is appropriate for the job. If discretion is an important requirement, though, directly ask about it—as in a behavioral question specifically addressing the candidate's skill in keeping private information confidential.

Robert: [out loud] Before we begin, Stephanie, I just wanted to share with you a little about our approach to interviewing. I'll be taking notes as we talk. It helps me recall our conversation in more detail later on.

Stephanie: No problem at all.

Robert: Great. The other thing that I want to explain is that we use what we call a "behavioral" interview style here. I'll be asking you for examples of your experience in several key areas. You can help me by giving specific examples. Do you have any questions before we begin?

Stephanie: No. Sounds good. Fire away.

Robert should share with Stephanie the general interview approach that he uses. This is helpful in "training" Stephanie on the fact that Robert seeks specific answers about Stephanie's experiences that are relevant to the job. This helps emphasize that she can "shine" best in the interview by relating specific, substantive details about how she demonstrated a particular skill or philosophy in the past.

Robert: Wonderful. Okay then. As you know, grammar and sentence structure are strongly emphasized in the ninth and 10th grades here. We realize that studying grammar is often a dry lesson. Can you tell me about any creative approaches in this area that you've taken in the past, especially a way in which you've brought it to life for students?" What has worked? What didn't work? And what did you learn from it? What would you suggest if a new colleague asked you for advice on this?

Interviewers should ask only one question at a time. In this case, Robert combines four or five questions, making it difficult for the candidate to remember and respond to each question appropriately.

Stephanie: Great questions. Okay, I'll take them one at a time. To start with, I do agree. Grammar is often very dry.

Robert: [to himself] That was a great question. I remember when I was starting out and struggled teaching grammar. I'll be interested to hear what she has to say. Oh—I think she started talking. I better pay attention to her answer.

Stephanie: Earlier in my career, after struggling through what even I thought were dull lessons with the ninth-graders I was teaching at the time, I had an idea for a "quiz show" to help the students with …

The interviewer must use active listening skills during the interview. Stephanie does a good job of starting to give a substantive answer, telling a story about a specific, relevant experience she has had in the past.

After the interview proceeded for another 30 minutes or so, Robert was ready to wrap things up.

Robert: Stephanie, we've covered a lot of ground today, and I appreciate your candid answers. I don't mind telling you that I've been very impressed. We'll finish our last interviews on Friday. We want to get our staffing plan in place for next year as quickly as possible—so we'll be in touch with you the middle of next week with our decision.

Robert: [to himself] Well, I'm glad I didn't get scared off by the way she opened the interview. Stephanie really impressed me with the depth of her experience and her self-awareness. She might be exactly what we're looking for.

Stephanie: So, how did I do?

Robert: I want to consult with the others you spoke with. However, if their impressions are anything like my own—well, it all looks very favorable.

Robert: [to himself] Always leave them on a high note, they say. Right? I've got to say, I think I did a good job with this one.

Stephanie: Thanks. I'm really excited about the opportunity. I hope to hear from you soon.

While rapport-building and maintaining goodwill are two critical elements of a successful hiring process, at the same time, it is important not to mislead or overstate the candidate's chances to be hired. In this case, Robert has gone too far. While he tries to be appropriately upbeat and complimentary, his comment "if their impressions are anything like my own …" has created the impression the job is virtually a lock to be offered to Stephanie. If this is still an open question behind closed doors at the school, it is best to say less rather than more. Otherwise, the candidate feels misled or "used" if he or she doesn't ultimately receive a job offer.

Step 14: Assess results of interviews

Assess interviews against the established specifications (i.e., job requirements and performance characteristics and expectations). Each interviewer should complete a written assessment of the interview as soon as possible after the session, while the facts are still fresh. For a tool that can help interviewers record their assessment in a consistent fashion, see the Interview Evaluation Form (see again Example 3.4).

Note that, while the interviewers are asked for substantive feedback on the candidate, the form does not ask them to vote on whether the candidate should be hired. The exact use of this feedback varies by school. Depending on its culture, some schools may grant each hiring team member a vote, with the candidate with the most votes being offered the position. However, in many schools, the School Head serves as the ultimate arbiter—gathering the feedback and insights of the hiring team, but making the final decision.

Step 15: Invite final candidate(s) for a guest teaching demonstration

For many schools, it's a traditional aspect of the hiring process to ask candidates to come on campus and demonstrate their teaching practice in the school's setting. This is an excellent way of viewing firsthand the candidate's skills—particularly his or her interaction with students. While the demonstration lesson is admittedly artificial, even under the best circumstances, it still provides the best opportunity for gaining a "live" look at the candidate's interactions and classroom presence.

Some schools choose to conduct guest teaching sessions as part of the initial on-campus interview rather than at the finalist stage. This may create scheduling challenges (because of the larger number of candidates in the early stage of the process). This is perfectly appropriate—and may serve as an early double-check mechanism to screen for candidates who interview well but teach poorly, or vice versa.

To position the teaching demonstration for the greatest possible success, the hiring team should take the following steps.

- Provide the candidates with clear expectations well before the demonstration lesson to allow adequate time for preparation. Specifically, describe what the school is looking for (e.g., creativity, engaging with students, leading class discussions) so they can plan their lessons accordingly.

- Play to each candidate's strengths (i.e., ask him or her to demonstrate a class in his or her specialty area) when this is possible within the context of the overall curriculum of the class to be visited.

- Keep in mind the need to have the various candidates teach equivalent classes (e.g., all honors sections in a high school, or the same subject in an elementary homeroom setting).

- Prepare the students appropriately by being transparent about the purposes of the class. As much as possible, have the guest's topic relate to the students' curriculum to ensure students are as focused and engaged as possible.

- Prepare the candidate properly, providing perspective on how the lesson fits into the class's regular curriculum, what students have worked on in the few days leading up to the lesson, etc.

- Allow time onsite for the candidate to prepare himself or herself before giving the class.

Step 16: Check professional references and conduct background verification on finalist candidate(s)

Depending on how closely the finalist candidates are rated after the guest teaching demonstration, the school may decide to check references and conduct background screening on multiple candidates (if two or more are closely rated). Or, the school may select only the finalist (if one is clearly above the others). In all cases, though, professional references (for qualitative, mission-appropriateness reasons) and background verifications (for legal, safety reasons) must be checked scrupulously before offering or confirming a position for a candidate.

There are important distinctions between "professional reference checks" and "background screening"—terms that are often (mis)used interchangeably, but which represent two distinct processes.

Professional Reference Checks

The candidate's professional references should be personally checked by the hiring manager (the person to whom the position reports). The purpose is to gain qualitative information about the candidate from supervisors and colleagues—i.e., those in the best position to assess the candidate's on-the-job skills and behaviors (see "Telephone Reference Check Script," Example 3.6). Candidates are ordinarily asked to provide names and contact information for three professional references who can discuss the candidate's performance (which may be supplemented by written reference letters, if available).

Example 3.6

| **Exempli Gratia Academy** |
| Telephone Reference Check Script (*Example*) |
| The following Reference Check Script is provided as a guide to the conversation. It focuses on the same Characteristics of Professional Excellence and Essential Expectations that were identified in Step 4 and have been guiding the hiring process throughout. |

Candidate: Annette Richardson

Opening: Upper School History Teacher

Reference: Samuel Andrews

School or Organization: Central Prep

Title: Chair, History Department

Telephone: 811-555-1212

1. In what capacity have you known this candidate?

Professional, for four years

2. Briefly describe the position the candidate is applying for. Question: "How do you feel the candidate would work in this role and environment, and why?"

Very well. Annette is highly committed to educating children on their role as global ambassadors. I believe that she will excel in your culture.

3. What would you list as the candidate's top three or four characteristics on the job?

Dependability, energy, perseverance, commitment

4. Tell me something about the candidate's on-the-job behavior and performance regarding:

Healthy learning community: Reported that Annette is considered to be one of the most supportive and engaged colleagues on the entire faculty, constantly being sought out for quiet, confidential guidance by peers.

Consistency and reliability: Early in her career, Annette was prone to giving too many "special exceptions" to students that inadvertently lowered standards. She has focused on becoming much more consistent in enforcing standards in recent years, an effort that has had positive results.

5. If you had to suggest one area, skill, or characteristic for the candidate to work on or enhance in the future, what would it be, and why?

Sometimes her passion can lead Annette to raise her voice with colleagues, which is interpreted as conflict or confrontation. Being mindful of this helps her be a better colleague.

6. Is there anything we haven't talked about that you feel would be pertinent if the candidate became an employee of our school?

Her extensive volunteer work with a global charity aligns closely with the school's mission.

Note: If the reference is a current or former supervisor (e.g., the teacher's current or past School Head), a closing question might be, "If you had the opportunity to rehire this individual, would you?"

Closing Statement: "Thank you for your time and consideration. Reference checking is an important part of our hiring process, and we appreciate your assistance a great deal."

Background Verification

Background verification involves confirming the information the candidate has provided about prior employment, education, criminal record, and driving record. Due to the requirements of the Fair Credit Reporting Act (FCRA) regarding use of information contained in background reports (see Appendix A), schools should contract with outside vendors for this service.

For the school's legal protection, tightly control background results. For example, the School Head or Division Head may be responsible for notifying the Business Manager that a background check should be ordered on a finalist candidate. The Business Manager would then order the appropriate report. Transmit the results—when received—directly to the individual at the school who is responsible for assessing whether the candidate's background meets the school's standards. This should be the school's Business Manager or HR professional. This position is outside the faculty hiring chain of command and is least susceptible to claims of using the background information for discriminatory purposes in the future, if the candidate is hired.

The hiring manager is informed solely of the candidate's "pass or fail" status. He or she is not given the reasons for the determination, for his or her own protection, as well as that of the candidate and the school.

Verification Reports

The school must determine the extent to which it checks the candidate's background. For example, perhaps the candidate has lived in three states in the past seven years. Will the school request the vendor check the criminal records in all three states, or just the last state of residence? The same question exists for motor vehicle records (assuming the faculty position requires driving—such as to and from field trips, athletic contests, and the like).

Ultimately, this becomes a risk management question for the school—determining the relative cost-benefit relationship between the safety of greater knowledge vs. the time and expense of securing more reports. Schools should develop a standard protocol. (See the Sample Criteria Chart, Example 3.7.) Review and modify these parameters based on the school's needs and interests.

Similarly, schools should establish criteria by which the screening report reviewer (e.g., the Business Manager or HR professional) can determine whether the candidate meets the school's standards concerning criminal history and other background report elements. The exact criteria used depends in large measure on the school's culture and values—i.e., its views on youthful transgressions and the question of forgiveness vs. the value of protecting its students, employees, and community members.

Example 3.7

Sample Criteria Chart			
Screening Report	**When Ordered**	**Parameters**	**Disqualifying Criteria** (unless significant mitigating circumstances)
Criminal	For all openings	Order national search plus sex offender registry check	Any convictions • for violent acts • involving fraud or embezzlement • requiring registration as a sex offender • for acts involving minors • for felonies in past seven years
Employment	For all openings	Check the last three employers (up to 10 years)	Any misrepresentation regarding dates of employment, position title, or duties
Education	For all openings	Verify the highest degree	Any material misrepresentation regarding completion of degree or type or level of degree
Motor Vehicle	For openings which driving for school business is an expectation	Check DMV records in state of current and past residences	Within the past 36 months: • three or more moving violations • any convictions for DWI/DUI

Reminders and Notes

- No references should be contacted nor any background reports ordered before the candidate signs a Background Screening Consent Form. Advise the hiring manager immediately about the screening outcome. If the candidate fails the screening, trigger the FCRA notification process.

- Federal and state agencies and laws are increasingly limiting the type and extent of background information that may be used in the hiring process (e.g., the use of credit checks and even criminal background checks is increasingly coming under scrutiny). Consult the school's employment attorney concerning current law.

- As social media continues to evolve, more employers are conducting internet searches on candidates, checking their public social media pages, etc., before inviting them for interviews. As this practice becomes more widespread, we are beginning to see court decisions on the legalities of using social media information in the hiring process. We caution all schools to consider the risks involved in obtaining potentially discriminatory information about a candidate (i.e., pertaining to protected characteristics such as race, ethnicity, and sexual orientation). Possessing such information may place the school at risk of a discrimination lawsuit should the candidate not receive an offer of employment. Schools should consult with their employment attorney before engaging in social media checks of this type.

Step 17: Select the final candidate

After all the interviewing, data-gathering (e.g., guest teaching), reference-checking, and background verification processes have concluded, the hiring team reconvenes to select the final candidate. As noted above, this process varies based on the School Head's desired approach. The Head may choose to have the hiring team:

- recommend a candidate for his or her approval;
- offer a small slate of candidates for the Head to select from; or
- select a candidate to be hired by "vote" or consensus.

No matter which process is used, all decision-makers (and all of those with input) consider all final candidates in terms of how they compare against the school's desired skills, experience, expectations, and characteristics of excellence. No hiring process is 100% foolproof. But continual references to mission, culture, and values when making hiring decisions are the best and most effective course for schools to take. When consistently applied, this ultimately leads the school to the faculty it seeks.

Step 18: Determine the job offer

On selection of the final candidate, the school can then determine the terms of the job offer. The offer must be consistent with the school's policies, salary structure, culture, and expectations.

Step 19: Make a verbal job offer to the finalist

Once the job offer is determined, the appointed administrator (usually the Division Head or School Head) calls the candidate with the job offer. Train the person making this call to avoid inadvertently making promises that can be construed as verbal contracts—e.g., "I'm sure we can revisit your salary needs after six months"—unless the promise will be included as an employment term in the offer letter or contract. By sticking to the terms approved by the Head, the school protects itself against making unintended contractual promises.

Candidates may accept "on the spot," or they may ask for a few days to consider the offer. The school should be clear with the candidate as to what it considers an acceptable time frame for response.

Step 20: On acceptance of an offer, issue the contract and notify nonselected candidates

When the candidate has verbally accepted the job offer, a written contract can be prepared. Then, notify all remaining candidates they have not been selected, to bring closure to the process and maintain goodwill. These qualified applicants may be top candidates for another opening next year.

ISM has developed the following Faculty Contract (Example 3.8). Sample contract language is shown in black. Commentary and "tips" are shown in italics within the contract.

Example 3.8

Exempli Gratia Academy
Faculty Contract (*Sample*)

THIS AGREEMENT is made and entered into by and between the School Head, as the duly authorized agent of Exempli Gratia Academy, Inc., a nonprofit corporation of the State of ____ (hereinafter called the "School") and NAME _____(hereinafter called the "Educator"). The parties agree as follows.

1. Term of Contract:

The School will employ the Educator for the 20__–20__ School Year, commencing August 15, 20__ and ending August 14, 20__. Both parties agree that neither the Educator nor the School owes any subsequent contractual obligation or services to the other after the ending date of this contract. There are no restrictions whatsoever on either party's right to choose to seek or refuse to seek another contract with the other party after the expiration of this agreement, and both parties are free to negotiate future employment on an equal basis.

2. Void Contract:

Should any existing employment contract between the parties be terminated before expiration, the contract set forth herein shall be null and void and neither party shall owe any compensation or services to the other.

Whether the school elects to use a 10- or 12-month contract (as referenced here), in all cases the starting and ending dates should be selected to include all dates on which the teacher's services are needed (i.e., the contract should start on or before the preschool orientation week and should end on or after the end-of-school meetings).

If the School has signed this contract for the next school year (i.e., starting in August or September) but then determines the teacher must be let go in the current year, this clause ensures the new contract is automatically voided before it goes into effect. (This avoids the messy situation where the school terminates someone but he or she still has a valid contract for next year, requiring the school to buy him or her out of a full year's salary).

3. Position and Duties:

The Educator is appointed to the position of _____ in the _____ division of the School. The Educator shall perform all reasonable duties as assigned by the School Head or his or her designee appropriate to the Educator's skills and position and as needed to fulfill the School's plans, programs, and standards. The Educator understands and agrees that he or she may be regularly called on to perform duties—including but not limited to cocurricular duties—that may often take place outside of what is generally considered to be the standard school day. The Educator agrees to attend all required meetings, keep all records, and prepare and file all reports customary for his or her position and as required and directed by the School.

4. Duty of Compliance:

The Educator agrees to perform these duties and consistently meet the School's Essential Expectations to the best of his or her abilities to the School's satisfaction, in accord with the laws of the State of _____, and complying with the policies and procedures of the School (as spelled out in the School's faculty and employee handbook and other relevant documents). In addition, the Educator agrees to abide by the rules, regulations, and requirements established by the Board of Trustees of the School. In any instance where the School's policies and procedures are deemed to be in conflict with the terms and conditions of this contract, the contract's terms and conditions shall take precedence.

The School may wish to list the Essential Expectations and specify particular classroom, coaching, and cocurricular duties within this section—or include an "addendum" (referenced and incorporated as part of the contract) that spells out duties and requirements in detail. However, schools should act with caution when spelling out duties too exactly. Few schools can predict the shifting operational needs that develop during the spring and summer after a contract has been signed. Thus, the School should avoid language that unnecessarily restricts it from changing the teacher's duties within reason if the needs of the School change. The School should explicitly reference the faculty and employee handbook policies and procedures, incorporating those policies and procedures as terms and conditions of the contract. In doing so, however, the School should review the faculty and employee handbook carefully to ensure that its policies are not in conflict with the provisions of this contract.

5. Compensation:

In consideration of the Educator's services (as set forth in this contract), the School agrees to pay the Educator the sum of $_____ during the term of this contract. Compensation shall be subject to all deductions and tax withholdings required by applicable federal, state, and local law.

Paid Time-Off: The Educator is eligible for ____ sick days and ____ personal days during the term of this contract. Use of sick and personal time is governed by provisions stated in the faculty and employee handbook.

The School may choose to specify here whether unused sick and personal days can be carried over to potential future contracts, or if unused sick and personal time is paid out at the conclusion of the contract. Alternatively, the School may choose to leave these details for the faculty and employee handbook.

Overtime Status: The Educator's position has been determined to be exempt from federal and state overtime regulations and thus he or she is not eligible to earn or be paid additional compensation (commonly referred to as "overtime") for additional hours worked. The Educator's compensation may be reduced by periods of unpaid leave or for other legally permissible reasons set forth by the School Head.

It is vital to clarify the exempt or nonexempt status of the teacher's position, so there is no confusion or dispute regarding eligibility for overtime pay. (Please note that a teacher, as an exempt employee, can only have his or her salary reduced or stopped for reasons permissible under FLSA.)

School Breaks: The Educator is paid his or her full salary during regularly scheduled school breaks (such as winter or spring break) when classes are not in session. The School shall pay the Educator over 10 months or 12 months at the Educator's election, in accord with the School's ordinary payroll practices. To comply with Section 409a of the IRS tax code, the Educator is required to complete a written election of his or her selection.

If the School permits the faculty member to choose to be paid over 12 months instead of 10, a written "election" is required to comply with Section 409a of the tax code (or else the school and the employee risks penalties on deferred compensation). A 12-month contract avoids this issue.

6. Benefits:

The Educator shall be permitted to participate in all employee benefits programs available to a teacher for which he or she otherwise qualifies, as per the guidelines of the plans that comprise the School's benefits offerings. The cost, if any, of participating in the employee benefits which the Educator elects will be deducted from the Educator's pay with his or her authorization, according to the established procedures of the School.

Some schools may choose to recite all the faculty member's benefits options in this section—or as an addendum to this contract. Where benefits plans are recited in detail, the School should be careful to add a clause to the contract indicating that, "While brief descriptions of the plans are provided here for summary purposes, the provisions of the official plan documents govern the administration and eligibility criteria of the plans. Where there is any discrepancy between these brief descriptions and the official plan documents, the terms of the official plan documents prevail."

The Educator understands that benefits plans may be created, modified, or eliminated from time to time, as permitted by law and the agreements between the School and its benefits providers—and that such changes may occur during the term of this contract. The Educator is eligible to participate in the benefits plans as per the then-current terms of the individual plans.

7. Confidentiality:

The Educator acknowledges that during the course of employment, he or she may obtain or have access to confidential information that is important to the School's business. This includes, but is not limited to, matters related to students, parents, employees, donors, and volunteers and may include student, parent, employee, volunteer, and donor names, academic records, addresses, financial information, and other personal information. The Educator may also become aware of marketing and academic plans and other information proprietary to the School. This is all herein referred to collectively as "Confidential Information." The Educator acknowledges that such Confidential Information is the property of the School. The Educator agrees that during the term of this Agreement and thereafter, for so long as the pertinent information remains confidential, the Educator shall not divulge or otherwise make use of any Confidential Information, directly or indirectly, personally, on behalf of any other person, business, organization, or entity, without the prior written consent of the School.

Include a similar confidentiality statement in the School's faculty and employee handbook.

8. New Employees:

If the Educator has not previously been employed by the School, this contract is contingent on the following:

The Educator must complete a full application for employment. The Educator represents and warrants that all the statements and facts set forth on the application are true and correct and there has been no omission of material facts therein. Any false or misleading statement(s) of material fact(s) in the application or omission of material fact(s) shall be grounds for termination of employment and concurrent voiding and termination of this contract.

By the time a contract is offered to a new employee, the School should have already ensured that an Application for Employment was completed and signed by the candidate—ordinarily at the time he or she was first interviewed on campus. Accepting a résumé only, without a signed application, provides insufficient protection for the School, as the candidate's résumé is not signed by the candidate and thus he or she is not certifying the accuracy of its contents.

The Educator must also successfully complete all requirements of the School's pre-employment screening process, including but not limited to: criminal background and/or fingerprint checks, reference checks, and pre-employment drug testing. The Educator understands and agrees the School may obtain consumer credit reports (commonly known as "background screening reports") for legally permissible screening purposes.

In compliance with the Fair Credit Reporting Act (FCRA), the School should also ensure that a Background Screening Authorization Form is completed by every candidate who is interviewed by the School.

9. Termination Provisions:

With the best interest of the School's students in mind, both parties intend for all aspects of the Educator's duties to be carried out for the full term of this contract. However, if grave circumstances or events compel one or both parties to seek to terminate this contract before its ending date, the following provisions apply:

It is vital the contract provide explicit termination provisions. If it does not, it may easily be construed the School must pay the teacher for the full term of the contract (even if it validly terminated the employee midyear for performance or behavior issues).

Educator Resignation: If the Educator desires to resign his or her position, the Educator must give thirty (30) days' written notice to the School Head. If the Educator successfully carries out his or her duties during the notice period, he or she will be compensated through the end of the notice period. If the Educator does not provide thirty days' notice, compensation terminates as of the Educator's last day worked.

The 30-day provision is recommended to avoid sudden, unexpected resignations, which may significantly disrupt the classroom and continuity of student education. As an incentive to faculty members to avoid sudden resignations, schools may wish to state that references will be withheld if proper notice is not provided by the faculty member.

The parties agree the School, at its sole discretion, may elect to pay the employee for the thirty-day notice period in lieu of the Educator working through the notice period.

Conversely, based on its culture and values, the School may determine that it will pay out the contract in full, regardless of whether the termination is for cause. In such a case, by leaving this provision in the contract, the School is placing itself in a position to execute a "Separation Agreement and General Release" when terminating the employee. The release—which provides protection against future discrimination or wrongful termination claims by the employee—is validly offered because it provides valuable "additional consideration" (in the form of pay for the remainder of the term) that is not otherwise required.

Educator Termination for Cause: If the School, at its sole discretion, determines that it will terminate the Educator's employment for cause (defined for purposes of this contract as behavior which brings disrepute on the School; insubordination; or actions which place the School's students, employees, parents, volunteers, or visitors in physical, emotional, or other danger), the School will provide written notice to the Educator of such termination. In this event, this contract and all compensation due to the Educator will terminate as of the last day worked.

The School may wish to list several more examples of for-cause reasons for termination. This clause is intended to protect the School from having to pay out the remainder of the contract by distinguishing for-cause terminations from dismissals (described further below).

Temporary or Permanent Discontinuance of Operations: If the School determines the need to cease operations temporarily or permanently for financial, operational, or safety reasons (such as due to enrollment decline, legal action, or unsafe conditions due to flood or earthquake), the School will notify the Educator in writing and shall continue the Educator's compensation for thirty (30) days beyond the last day worked or thirty days beyond the date of written notice, whichever is later.

Educator Dismissal: If the School, at its sole discretion, determines the need to terminate the Educator's employment for reasons other than those outlined above, the school will provide written notice to the Educator and shall continue the Educator's compensation through the end of the term of this contract.

As noted above, the School may determine it is most consistent with its culture and values to pay a terminated employee in full when dismissing a faculty member midyear. As the School doesn't want inadvertently to create (or deny) benefits termination or continuation rights that are different from existing practices and federal and state COBRA laws, it should review all benefits provisions in the contract carefully.

Termination of Employee Benefits: In all cases in which this contract is terminated before the end of its term, the Educator's ability for employee benefits provided by the School shall terminate according to the regular provisions of the School's employee benefits programs.

10. Ability to Enter into Contract:

The Educator hereby affirms that he or she is not under contract with any other school covering a part or all the same period as contemplated by this contract, nor is he or she bound by any other restriction preventing him or her from legally entering this binding contract.

This affirmation is intended to prevent the teacher from entering contracts in violation of existing contractual terms (e.g., signing a contract with one School in March after having previously signed a contract with another school in February for the coming school year).

11. Entire Agreement, Modifications, and Severability:

Both parties expressly acknowledge that this contract expresses the only agreement between the parties hereto, unmodified and unaffected by any other understanding whatsoever. Any other perceived representation by the Educator or the School (including its agents or employees)—except for written documents explicitly incorporated by reference into this contract, such as the School's faculty and employee handbook—are not part of this contract or contractual representations. This contract may only be modified in writing, signed by the Educator and the School Head (or his or her designee), and titled, "Modification of Contract."

Should any provision of this contract be invalidated by a court of law with proper jurisdiction, the remaining provisions shall remain in full force and effect.

These are standard legal provisions in most contracts.

12. Jurisdiction:

The parties agree that this contract shall be interpreted in accordance with the laws of the State of _____, and the venue for any action concerning this contract shall be the state or federal court having jurisdiction over these matters in the County of _____.

Similarly, this is a standard legal provision.

In consultation with its legal counsel—and depending on its philosophy—the School may elect to specify that contract claims will be mediated by an arbitrator (rather than through a court proceeding). Schools should consult with legal counsel to determine if a mandatory arbitration clause is permissible or advisable under their state's laws.

13. Modification and Expiration of Contract Offer:

The School reserves the right to modify or rescind the above offer of employment before acceptance by the Educator.

This contract offer shall be null and void unless the Educator returns an executed copy of this contract to the School by _____ (date), unless this deadline is extended in writing by the School Head or his or her designee.

For practical purposes, most schools need to have contracts signed (or declined) by specific deadlines so that hiring vacancies can be addressed in a timely manner.

Signatures and Dates

Name _____ Date _____

Note: ISM's Sample Faculty Contract (above) should never be used as is. This sample is provided for discussion purposes only. All contracts and other legal documents should be drafted and reviewed by an employment attorney qualified in the school's specific state or jurisdiction.

Step 21: Receive the signed contract

On receiving the signed contract, the school needs to:

- close out the recruiting file, and
- create an individual personnel file for the employee.

Recruiting File

The school should maintain a recruiting file that contains a complete record of the recruiting process for the position, including:

- the Faculty Job Description and Hiring Specifications Form or equivalent (see again Example 3.1);
- the recruitment advertising and job posting;
- all résumés received;
- all applications for employment (copies) and consent forms (copies) received from candidates who interviewed for the position; and
- interview notes and comments in the form of completed Interview Planning and Evaluation Forms from all members involved in the interviewing process.

Maintain this file for two years after the completion of the hiring process (i.e., two years after the position is filled or a decision not to fill is made).

Personnel File

The school should establish individual personnel files for all new employees containing:

- application for employment (original);
- background screening consent form (original);
- résumé; and
- employment contract.

All other recruiting-related forms pertaining to the position and not the employee (such as the Faculty Hiring Specifications Form) should remain in the recruiting file for the position.

Once the employee is hired and begins working, numerous additional documents will be entered into the individual's personnel file, including:

- I-9 form,
- W-4 (payroll and taxation) form,
- performance evaluations, and
- employment contracts for subsequent years.

To comply with myriad regulations pertaining to different aspects of personnel records (such as maintaining performance evaluations until discrimination claim statutes of limitations expire), schools should maintain personnel files for seven years after the employee terminates employment with the school.

Step 22: Launch the Orientation and Induction processes

ISM knows that almost 50% of teachers new to the profession leave within the first five years, and the average annual turnover rate for teachers in private schools is around 20%. The two major reasons for teacher turnover are compensation issues and lack of administrative support.

An effective orientation to the school's policies, processes, culture, and mission is important for ensuring that all employees get off to a good start with the school. A comprehensive and sustained induction process helps a new faculty member acclimate to—and use his or her full skills within—the school's mission, culture, and values much more quickly and effectively than would otherwise be the case. This is the topic of the following chapter.

Summary

A mission-based hiring process is admittedly an intensive one—requiring substantial commitments of time, energy, and reflection of the School Head and his or her Leadership Team. Yet, given the central role that faculty plays in the school's long-term viability and the successful delivery of mission to students, it is vital that all concerned approach the process with the greatest vigor and dedication possible.

While no process for hiring succeeds 100% of the time, the mission-based approach is designed to give schools the greatest likelihood of hiring mission-appropriate teachers in every possible case.

Mission-Based Onboarding: Orientation and Induction

The process of introducing a new teacher to the school and its norms and expectations includes orientation and induction. Some schools mistakenly see the two as synonymous, thereby overlooking induction or treating it as an afterthought, as opposed to a critical component of the teacher's successful career at their school.

Consulting dictionary.com, we find:

- *orientation (noun)*: an introduction, to guide one in adjusting to new surroundings, employment, activity, or the like: *"New employees receive two days of orientation."*

- *induction (noun)*: Origin: late 14th century, from *inductionem* (Latin), noun of action from *inducere* (to lead)

These definitions give us insight into the important differences between orientation and induction processes. As a practical matter, we see this distinction clearly when comparing traditional New Teacher Orientation meetings (one-time, multiday event at the beginning of each school year), and New Teacher Induction (a systematic growth and support plan implemented over the course of two years, incorporating various processes designed to support teacher growth).

We view orientation as a part of induction, but the process doesn't end there. The New Teacher Orientation meetings are an important kickoff to the induction process, but in essence it is exactly what the name implies: a one-time orientation event. If this event represents the sum total of the school's induction efforts, it falls far short of its potential impact on the life of the new teacher and the life of the school.

Rather, orientation should be only the beginning of what is ideally an 18- to 24-month sequence of events designed to effectively inculcate the new teacher into the culture and norms of the school. (This is articulated in large measure by the mission statement, Characteristics of Professional Excellence (CPE), and Portrait of the Graduate (POG) documents referenced earlier—see Chapter Two for details.) Below we examine the essential components of each process.

Onboarding Mentors

Assign an onboarding mentor to each teacher before the orientation days, which are held just before the start of the school year. Ideally, mentors are exemplary faculty members who are excited to guide and facilitate the induction process for new teachers.

Note: for the purposes of onboarding, we use the term "onboarding mentor" to distinguish it from the coach or mentor who assists faculty in developing their professional growth. In this chapter we often shorten "onboarding mentor" to simply "mentor." It should be noted that the onboarding mentor, after the orientation and induction process (first year) is complete, does not necessarily continue in the role of coach or mentor in subsequent years.

The role of the onboarding mentor is to:

- be a nonjudgmental listener available to answer any questions the mentee may have (or guide him or her to someone who has the answer);
- offer suggestions and resources; and
- help plan and attend induction meetings throughout the year.

For hires who are new to teaching, it is often best to have a mentor within the same department. For experienced teachers new to the school, the mentor may be from another department and be matched according to personality and interests. If timing allows, provide opportunities for the mentor and mentee to meet before orientation. The onboarding mentor could take the new teacher on a tour, familiarizing him or her with the school's essential areas and resources (e.g., copy room, the teacher's classroom[s], faculty room, restrooms, cafeteria, nurse, IT).

Orientation

A common mistake schools make in designing orientation days is to try to cover everything teachers may need to know over the course of the year. This not only overwhelms the teachers and causes unnecessary anxiety, but much of the information is likely to be forgotten. The orientation should instead focus on welcoming new teachers into the community and providing the information and resources that are immediately relevant and necessary at the start of the year. Shift other items from orientation to the induction process so the content is presented when it becomes necessary to perform the task at hand. The induction calendar is designed to provide teachers with the information they need at specific points in the year.

Community Building

The first and most critical component of orientation is welcoming and community building. Ensure that all new faculty members are introduced to the rest of the teachers and warmly welcomed. This may be done by the Head, Division Head, Department Chair, or mentor, depending on what fits best with the school's culture and traditions. Ideally the person chosen to introduce has an opportunity to interview the new teacher to personalize the introduction.

Generic: "This is John Smith. He's joining our math department and will be teaching algebra II and geometry."

Personalized: "This is John Smith. He just moved here from Springfield with his wife, Carrie, and his two schnauzers, Max and Tippy. In fact, the moving truck was late so he just got finished unpacking sometime after midnight last night! Thank you, John, for making such an effort to be here this morning. John got his B.A. in math and M.S. in educational cognitive science from Sample University. He taught at Exempli Gratia Academy for 11 years, and now we're fortunate enough to have him joining our math department, teaching algebra II and geometry. He'll be in rooms 241 and 234, so make sure you stop by and say 'hi'. If you get a chance, ask him about his harrowing experience with a caribou in Alaska!"

Once teachers have been introduced, engage the full faculty in a brief icebreaker activity. While the term "icebreaker" can invoke groans and eye rolls, this activity serves an important purpose. It bonds the group in a common activity that typically results in laughter and learning something new about others. To maximize participation and effectiveness, solicit a group of teachers to choose, plan, and lead the activity.

Next, provide an opportunity for the new teachers to have meaningful conversations with their colleagues. For example, you may have interdisciplinary or interdivisional groups of six to eight per table discussing the year's guiding core value, or brainstorming teaching strategies that turn more of the learning over to students. If this process is planned and led by teachers, all the better.

Preparation for the Start of the Year

Once new teachers have been brought into the community, they need to know what to do and how to do it. While each school, division, and department may be different in terms of the tools and resources, teachers need to start the year with confidence. Consider this list of potential topics and activities.

- Tour of the school
- Review of Essential Expectations (which would have been communicated during the interview and hiring process)
- Introduction to key staff members who may be needed within the first weeks of school (e.g., IT, librarians, nurse)
- Time to meet with other new hires in their induction cohort
- Time to set up classroom(s)
- Time to meet with mentor and departments
- Time to plan the first week of classes in collaboration with peers
- Classroom management strategies (for those new to teaching)
- Tutorial on a school-provided laptop and software (e.g., gradebook, email, school portal)
- Tutorial on any instructional technology teachers are expected to use
- Review of the most critical elements of the faculty and employee handbook (save the rest for induction)
- Glossary of school-specific terminology and acronyms
- Attendance-keeping protocol

- ▪ Advisory: objectives, advisor role, and advisory meeting structure
- ▪ Legal or HR requirements (varies by state)

Consult with teachers who have been at the school one to two years to determine which of these activities and topics (and others not on this list) are of most use to new teachers. Newer teachers best remember "what they wish they had known," and this is also a way to give them leadership roles.

Celebration

Orientation-opening meetings week should culminate in a celebration for all faculty and staff members that matches the school's culture and resources. This could range from coffee and cake to wine and cheese to a potluck picnic with all employees and their families invited. The culminating celebration has two objectives. The first is to provide a fun, community-building event that reminds teachers why they love the school and gives them an opportunity to unwind and get excited for the start of the year. The second is to express gratitude for the tremendous impact the teachers will have on students in the coming year.

Induction

A true induction program draws its purpose from the origin of the word "induction" shown above—that is to lead the new teacher into the life of his or her chosen vocation and profession, and into the life of the school.

When carried out systematically and with intentionality, an induction program maximizes and accelerates a new faculty member's chances of long-term success within the school. Induction experts observe that schools with effective induction programs produce teachers who:

- – feel (and are) well supported;
- – have a clear view of the values, norms, and processes of the school;
- – are more likely to establish ongoing peer networks; and
- – are much more likely to be enthusiastic (bonded) to the school in meaningful ways for extended periods of time (even lifelong).

Special acknowledgment: ISM acknowledges induction experts Harry Wong and Annette Breaux, authors of *New Teacher Induction: How to Train, Support, and Retain New Teachers* (Harry K. Wong Publications, 2003) and primary influencers of our thinking on induction.

Inducting New Teachers

Your New Teacher Induction program has two primary audiences.

1. Teachers who are new to the profession of teaching
2. Teachers who are new to your school, but are not new to the profession of teaching

For induction purposes, the main differences between these two groups are time and emphasis. New teachers (i.e., those coming to the school directly from undergraduate or graduate programs or who are making career changes into the teaching profession) should have a systematic induction program that lasts two years—or even three. These programs should encompass guidance on all aspects of teaching in and out of the classroom (e.g., advisory, club work, coaching, parent relations and internal marketing, time and stress management, and service learning). In terms of core skills, place special emphasis on classroom management and parent relations (two nonnegotiable skills for private school teachers).

Depending on available resources, these programs may include:

– model classrooms;

– regular peer observation;

– group interaction and reflection;

– significant readings and discussions of those readings; and

– general and skill-specific mentoring relationships.

Schools should consider increasing the frequency of periodic reviews as part of an effective induction program for these new professionals to ensure they are meeting the Essential Expectations of a faculty member. In addition, it is helpful that their coach is highly skilled at providing support and encouragement on an ongoing basis. New teachers need the best coaching for at least the first two years. This support must come from school leaders and peers.

As a practical matter, administrators must recognize there is a tension that exists for academic leaders related to a teacher's first two years. On one hand, new teachers need heavy doses of encouragement, skill building, and guidance to learn and negotiate the private school culture—i.e., support. On the other hand, effective administrators realize they must also use this time span to determine whether the new teacher is in fact a good fit with both school and profession—i.e., evaluation.

This tension between the need to provide high support and careful evaluation and assessment is particularly acute during the first two years. To resolve this, schools are wise, when staffing allows, to have the new faculty member's eventual coach (after his or her onboarding mentor has completed the year) be someone different than the supervisor. This helps reduce that tension.

Inducting Experienced Teachers Who Are New to the School

While the orientation of experienced teachers is the same as those new to the field (i.e., participating in beginning-of-year meetings), induction for these teachers is significantly different from those just beginning. The primary difference is a much more accelerated move toward an individualized growth plan in the first year.

While the focus for teachers new to the field is to cover classroom basics in detail, with experienced teachers new to your school the emphasis is on:

- determining if there are any concerning weaknesses and remediating those as soon as possible; and

- inculcating them as an individual into the school's mission, culture, values, and norms.

Thus, experienced teachers have a far more individualized program, which is worked out between the teacher and the administrator within the first month of school and adjusted as needed. Experienced teachers ordinarily should take no more than a single year to effectively acclimate to the school's culture.

The emphasis here is ensuring they make the transition from the missions, values, and norms of their prior school(s) to those of their new school. This means that much of the work with these teachers may include "un-teaching" approaches and behaviors that were acceptable (or even encouraged or required) at their prior school but which are misaligned with the new school's needs and expectations.

Returning to the theme of predictability and supportiveness, what this looks like is determined by the school's unique mission, culture, and values. In one school, teachers may be expected to ensure that students come to class in uniform, stand up when an adult enters the room, and address all adults as Mr. or Mrs. or Ms. In another school, there may be a relaxed dress code and a much more casual approach to student-teacher relationships (with students referring to teachers by their first name).

A teacher can excel in one context or culture and fail in another. Your induction program must support experienced teachers in making the transition from their former context to the new culture. Have academic leaders support teachers by being clear about what is or is not expected (and enforced) at the school.

Ideally, the careful interviewing process screened out candidates who would not successfully make this transition to being a fit for the school.

A Sample Two-Year Induction Calendar

In planning a New Teacher Induction program, use this sample as a guide. Schools must inevitably personalize their induction plan to reflect the school's calendar, events, and traditions.

The sample calendar below assumes the following.

- The onboarding mentor is assigned to a new hire for the first 18 months.
- The first two professional growth goals (develop effective classroom management and learn the skills for strong parent relations) are driven by the school.
- In the spring of the first year, assuming one of the two initial goals has been largely achieved, another goal (which replaces the achieved goal) is formulated based on a Characteristic of Professional Excellence.
- The first year includes two formal period reviews. (See Chapter Eight.)
- A new coach, who carries forward with the teacher, will be assigned in year two.
- The new hire's first self-directed growth plan is developed after 18 months.
- Following year two, the new teacher is on the same growth and evaluation cycles as veteran teachers.

Year One

- **August:** Welcome back meetings for all the faculty, New Teacher Orientation, assignment of onboarding mentor, model classroom exercises, determination of professional development goals with the onboarding mentor.
- **September:** New teacher workshop (effective classroom management), mentor visits to help implementation of ideas garnered from the classroom management workshop.
- **October:** New teacher reading and reflection group (e.g., reading on parent relations), teacher observes mentor or other peer teacher conduct a role play parent conference. Explanation of Pumpkin Festival tradition.
- **November:** Planned conversation with coach to plan for parent conferences. Workshop on writing personalized comments.

- **January:** First formal periodic review (conversations regarding EE may have already taken place as needed).

- **February:** New teacher reading and reflection group (e.g., fair and effective assessments), peer observation.

- **March:** New teacher reading and reflection group (e.g., fair and effective assessments). Explanation of March Madness tradition.

- **April:** Mentor assists in reviewing assessments and plans for culminating assessments.

- **May:** Second formal periodic review. Multiple end-of-year celebratory events with accolades for new faculty members.

Year Two

- **August:** New year, new teacher meeting (review of classroom management and parent relations and communications from last year). New coach assigned. Growth goals reviewed.

- **September:** Coach invited to observe classroom to help implementation of ideas garnered from peer observations.

- **October:** Ongoing conversations with coach.

- **November:** New teacher reading and reflection group (e.g., homework that really works).

- **January:** Planned review of professional growth goals progress. Last year's onboarding mentor and this year's coach help guide reflection for the new hire's first self-directed professional growth and renewal cycle.

- **April:** Formal periodic review, new teacher reading and reflection group, peer observation.

- **May:** Professional growth plan for next year developed. Multiple end-of-year celebratory events with accolades for new faculty members.

Summary

Thoughtfully segueing from the hiring process into a well-planned, 18- to 24-month induction program gives a school the best opportunity possible for keeping energetic new hires engaged, aligned, and passionate about delivering the school's mission every day.

Orienting to a New Approach to Growth and Evaluation

"Faculty quality" is a major reason families choose to enroll and re-enroll at a particular school. The school administration must adopt a process to ensure the school has hired, developed, and retained the best teachers. For decades, schools have looked to teacher evaluation models to help achieve this goal.

From the Frederick Taylor-inspired Scientific Method, to the Clinical Supervision improvement in the '60s, culminating with Charlotte Danielson's seminal 1996 work *Enhancing Professional Practice,* the 20th century proved to be a particularly generative time for ideas and approaches to teacher supervision and evaluation.

Though progress has been made, many teacher evaluation systems in use today struggle to serve their two primary purposes: accountability and improvement. The result has been nearly no success in either domain. A 2009 study titled *The*

Widget Effect (referenced earlier) heavily criticized teacher evaluation practices in the United States, concluding that nothing short of a complete overhaul of the teacher evaluation process was needed.

The study determined that, using current systems, "Excellent teachers cannot be recognized or rewarded, chronically low-performing teachers languish, and the wide majority of teachers performing at moderate levels do not get the differentiated support and development they need to improve as professionals."

While commending earlier efforts to develop fair and balanced evaluation approaches, ISM believes that current models do not accurately discriminate between effective and ineffective teachers, nor do they drive professional development or improve student outcomes.

Where do so many well-meaning efforts go wrong? As outlined in this book's introduction, ISM's approach to evaluation has evolved based on extensive experience and targeted research. We have found the following factors to be the primary **obstacles to success**.

1. **Leaders are unclear with their faculty.** ISM research found more than one in three teachers don't understand how leaders assess their performance (34.5% reported they did not agree with the item from ISM's Faculty Experience Survey [see Chapter 10], "I and my colleagues understand exactly how we are evaluated").

2. **Schools change their systems too often.** Nearly four in 10 teachers find the process inconsistent (39% did not agree that "I and my colleagues view our evaluation procedures as consistent [i.e., predictable]"). In schools with high administrator turnover, new leaders come in with new initiatives. Over time, faculty members may realize this pattern and be tempted to "wait it out," knowing the system will change again, so there is no real motivation to invest time in it.

3. **Many evaluation systems are too complex.** Evaluation systems often consist of numerous pages of rubrics and checklists, presumably to increase their potential reliability and validity. In an effort to be comprehensive, however, they become unwieldy and impossible for administrators to manage on an annual basis for each teacher.

4. **Administrators lack the time.** The primary responsibility of an academic administrator is to increase the capacity of the faculty. However, these administrators are extremely busy. Beyond their official job descriptions, there are any number of unanticipated fires to put out that

have the potential to disrupt their focus on what matters most. Most Division Heads ISM has worked with can't imagine being able to spend the recommended 25%–50% of their weekly time on faculty development. Accordingly, attention must be paid to the number of teachers each administrator is expected to evaluate (which is why, in many schools, Department Chairs are taking on more supervisory roles), and dedicated time for evaluating and coaching faculty members needs to be explicitly placed in the calendar and protected.

5. **Systems don't distinguish between effective and ineffective teachers.** The Widget Effect study disrupted prior conceptions of evaluation systems with the finding that performance evaluations result in the oxymoron of virtually all teachers being rated as "above average." The result is that excellence goes unrecognized and poor performance goes unaddressed.

6. **Formal classroom *observations* are confused with *evaluation*.** Related to the factor above, many schools still consider one or two formal classroom observations to be their evaluation process. When administrators visit teachers' classrooms, it should be to observe teaching and learning, coaching and mentoring. This is part of growth. If observation is the basis of evaluation, teachers will be afraid to try new things or take risks for fear of getting a bad evaluation should their administrator see a new strategy fail.

7. **Teachers are not perceived as excellent professionals.** ISM often asks administrators, "What do you believe about your faculty?" Some evaluation systems are based on the (perhaps unconscious) belief that unless teachers are strictly monitored, they won't perform. This leads to more time being spent on checklists and rules than on quality conversations about teaching and learning. We assert that schools must adopt a model that reflects the belief that most teachers are top-notch professionals who are "good" today and are constantly striving to be better tomorrow. If division leaders can't say each of their teachers is "good," then leadership must choose to selectively retain only those for whom that is true.

8. **Evaluation is confused with growth.** Research demonstrates that administrator-assessed teacher evaluation is not a mechanism to drive teacher growth for most teachers. The reason is that the remediation or "medical model" pervades the extant evaluation systems. Even if evaluators could spend enough time to objectively assess all teachers on the perfect set of criteria for teaching excellence, the process is designed for the evaluators to identify the teacher's deficits (i.e., the disease) and then prescribe a cure.

Given that in almost all areas teachers are rated as "above average" or "meets expectations," what growth is possible? Why would a teacher be directed to improve in an area in which he or she already meets expectations? If teachers meet expectations and improvement is still needed, then the school's expectations are too low. Further, when some authority prescribes a cure to some deficit, this casts the improvement as a compliance exercise— which incidentally is how most teachers perceive professional development directives. Better, more lasting growth occurs when the people doing the growing are intrinsically motivated to perpetually improve their practice— not because it results in a rating of "exceeds expectations" next year, but because they believe it helps students.

The competitive nature of private schools requires faculty members and administrators to be laser-focused on enhancing student performance, satisfaction, and enthusiasm. This requires schools to think differently about managing teacher performance. The first step to thinking differently is to understand the administration's primary goal is not to identify who is a good teacher and who is not, but to grow the entire faculty's capacity to positively affect students' success.

This understanding is accompanied by the realization that the "evaluation" component must be less prominent than the "growth" component in any system. Many components of a traditional evaluation system have repeatedly been shown to undermine the factors necessary for growth (predictability, support, trust, accuracy, locus of control). Schools must take the next step of uncoupling the evaluation cycle from the growth cycle (see Chapter One for models), running each with separate goals, procedures, and timelines. Chapter Six outlines the Growth and Renewal Cycle, while Chapter Seven reviews the Evaluation Cycle in detail.

Shared Foundational Beliefs

The success of the separation of the growth and evaluation cycles will be evident in its implementation. School leadership must be responsible for creating the environment where this uncoupling is felt by the faculty, instead of just talked about by administrators. In fact, if the faculty does not recognize the separation, the entire process is undermined. To achieve this environment, leaders must adopt the following critical beliefs.

- All teachers are "good" today but unequivocally must be better tomorrow.
- The locus of control for each faculty member's growth must rest with the teachers, and they must direct developing their learning goals. Leaders must also resist the trap of being too directive and thus wrestling the locus of control away from the faculty. Similarly, they must resist any

passive-aggressive efforts on the part of faculty members to hand it back, expecting leadership to tell them what they should improve.

■ Professional development is not an event, but an integral part of the weekly and daily experience of teachers as they plan lessons and experiences for students. Goals and progress will be in a continuous cycle rather than a yearly one.

■ Teachers are professionals who—through review of data and feedback, reflection, and working with others (peers and leaders)—determine the right goals for their development.

■ A new approach that was designed to improve student learning but did not work as well as planned is not a failure. Instead it is evidence of engagement in the continuous process of development, provided the teacher reflects, redesigns, and tries again.

Dual Processes, Dual Responsibilities, Dual Roles

Given that CFD intentionally splits the evaluation and growth cycles into two separate processes, it is important to identify the separate roles and responsibilities supervisors may play in their application. In the process of facilitating faculty growth, a supervisor would serve as a coach or mentor, perceiving how he or she needs to "be" to get the most out of the faculty member. Whereas, in the process of completing the formal periodic evaluation, the supervisor must become a judge, assessing the teacher's performance against the Essential Expectations (EE). The supervisors' roles carry with them different responsibilities and different "ways of being."

Coaching and Mentoring Defined

The dictionary provides us with definitions of coaching and mentoring as nouns and verbs.

> *Coach:* (n.) a person who trains an athlete or a team; (v.) to give instruction or advice

> *Mentor:* (n.) a wise and trusted counselor; (v.) to influence, sponsor, and support

We do not distinguish between the two terms, but rather see them as a combined idea. The coach or mentor is someone who:

– trains the teacher (particularly in the case of those new to the profession);

– listens carefully before giving advice or direction;

– asks probing questions that drive deep thought and problem-solving;

– helps teachers see "the big picture" and understand where they fit into it;

– is trusted (credible) and wise (takes a long view of events);

– gives honest feedback in a helpful fashion;

– knows the person well enough to determine what elicits renewal and motivation;

– encourages (influences) the teacher and builds his or her confidence (supports); and

– functions as a success agent (sponsor) for the teacher, providing resources, people, materials, and information that aid the teacher's growth and development.

In practical terms, this can be reduced to two key aspects. That is, the administrator as coach or mentor communicates expectations and provides guidance, support, encouragement, and resources necessary to attain expectations.

In fulfilling these roles, the mentor's primary responsibility is to serve as a trusted voice and to be there for that teacher. Through an ongoing conversation, mentors must develop a strong working relationship that invites the faculty member to expand his or her abilities and approaches to best serve students.

Said differently, a coach must be an agent for positive change. To do so, he or she must embody the necessary qualities of an effective helper: warmth, authenticity, and empathy. The faculty members should feel each coach has general positive regard toward them (warmth) and respects them for their uniqueness and current approach to teaching. A coach must be "genuine," acting and expressing emotions in congruence with who he or she truly "is." Mentors must also be able to put themselves in the shoes of the mentee (empathy) and communicate that through his or her responses and demeanor.

It is vital that a coach be trained and become skilled in the coach or mentor role. It is not easy for many people. Some struggle with learning to listen or being overly directive, while others are good listeners but are afraid to provide honest feedback. Professional development and practice (e.g., role-playing ongoing conversations) are essential to being an effective coach.

It is equally vital the School Head and the Leadership Team organize the school's processes, schedules, and resources to enable this relationship to occur. Time, perhaps the most important resource here, must be spent and scheduled for teachers and mentors to have these conversations. If the strategy for creating time for these conversations is "to find time as we can," that is a losing approach.

Schedule and use the time. It should not be discarded when schedules get busy. If a sense of of "this time is not as important as our 'regular responsibilities'" is perceived by the community, it undermines the entire process.

If the coach is executing this role with excellence, then it is highly likely that mission-appropriate, competent teachers respond positively to the coaching and mentoring, and grow and thrive.

Evaluator

While the ultimate responsibility for an evaluator and a mentor or coach is to the school's mission and the students it serves, their roles are different. The coach works with the teacher—his or her "client"—fostering growth and development. The evaluator, on the other hand, completes the periodic review *for* the school, ensuring every faculty member is meeting the Essential Expectations and job responsibilities.

The effective evaluator:

- is adept at creating a faculty culture with high levels of predictability and support;
- communicates expectations and job responsibilities to all;
- is frequently visible in the community in the halls and classrooms and at events;
- memorizes the Essential Expectations (see Chapter Seven);
- accurately recognizes expressions of the Essential Expectations;
- takes notes regarding any remarkable examples of the Essential Expectations and any alarming issues;
- follows up on potential issues to get a complete picture (vs. letting hearsay overly influence assessment); and
- is fair and predictable when applying the need for corrective action.

Most communities know who is and is not meeting Essential Expectations, through the individual's attitude, words, and actions. ISM Consultants collectively interview thousands of faculty members each year, often spending fewer than 30 minutes with any one teacher. Through those short meetings, Consultants can usually identify the "star" and the toxic teachers. Well-crafted and well-communicated Essential Expectations, duties, and responsibilities should make the evaluation process easy to complete.

A Note About Dual Relationships

It is critical that all involved understand fully the dual roles of the academic administrator as evaluator and coach or mentor. ISM repeatedly hears administrators voice their concerns with the duality of the role—convinced that if they engage in critical evaluation, the teacher will never accept them as a coach.

Unfortunately, this is true in a fair number of cases. It's particularly problematic for administrators who are poor at creating a predictable and supportive environment, as they invite fears and uncertainty among the faculty. ISM has intentionally separated the growth and evaluation cycles primarily because evidence suggests that it is difficult for people to trust that supervisors can compartmentalize their roles completely.

As a result, ideally the evaluator and the coach or mentor roles are divided between different people as well. By separating growth from the evaluation process, coaching and mentoring can be shared across many different roles, apart from supervising administrators (e.g., peers, Department Chairs, Deans). However, sometimes an administrator must still take on dual roles with faculty members. The success of the coach or mentor role hinges on the administrator's ability to craft a relationship built on predictability and support that engenders high levels of trust.

To address this dilemma, we suggest that administrators imagine their role as similar to that of the most student-supportive teachers in the school. These are teachers who confidently go about assessing the quality of student work, insisting on high standards, while always being clearly "on the students' side."

Similarly, the evaluator role calls for an administrator to examine the teacher's contributions to the life of the school, while acting as a coach or mentor supporting the teacher's work. This is all with the institutional mission and its implications as the overriding standard against which all faculty members must be measured.

Supervisors who are most successful at navigating the dual roles:

- constantly emphasize the purpose common to both roles: continuous improvement to better deliver the school's mission and enhance student success;

- are excellent mentors, knowing how to engage in the ongoing conversation without being overly directive;

- overtly demonstrate positive regard, genuineness, and empathy toward all faculty members;

- openly identify the conflict in the dual roles with the faculty member and encourage conversations about it; and

– maintain fairness when deciding to rate a faculty member as not meeting expectations, placing the teacher in corrective action.

If the school has more than 15 faculty members, the Division Head cannot mentor them all, because of time constraints. As a result, some dual-role overlap occurs. Perhaps avoid having the Division Head coach a new faculty member or a teacher who has had difficulty meeting Essential Expectations in the past. This may seem counterintuitive—isn't it important for the top supervisor to work with these teachers? However, consider that it may be necessary to work through more directive coaching with faculty members in these categories, and keeping the relationships as clean as possible is advantageous.

Note also the CFD evaluation process was intentionally designed to reduce the burden many evaluation systems place on supervisors. As Chapter Seven discusses, the Essential Expectations should be important but obvious and less contentious. A simple "meeting expectations" or "not meeting expectations" was intended to reduce the tenor of the evaluation process to something easily classified as "no secrets, no surprises." In other words, the predictability level should remove much of the potential conflict arising from dual roles.

ISM encourages School Heads to have candid conversations about the evaluator-coach dichotomy with any potential administrators before hiring them for the role. For those who are already in place and are struggling to reconcile the duality, they may simply need to seek a different position from which to contribute their talents.

The Question of Subject-Specific Coaching

Teachers and administrators alike may question a mentor's ability to work with teachers outside his or her discipline or specialty (e.g., an administrator whose background is in history mentoring a chemistry teacher). Two considerations come into play.

1. A skilled administrator's coaching or mentoring focuses on teaching techniques and approaches that transcend any discipline (i.e., by helping this person reinforce the principles of predictability and supportiveness).

2. The "success agent" part of the administrator's role comes to the fore here, as well.

It is unnecessary for the administrator to be the individual mentoring the teacher directly. Rather, the administrator may broker the teacher's growth by arranging for discipline-appropriate guidance (such as arranging for a veteran science teacher or the Department Chair to mentor the chemistry teacher on science-specific teaching techniques, approaches, etc.).

Coaching and Mentoring the Coaches and Mentors

School Heads have an important role in the Comprehensive Faculty Development Model. They are called on to coach the Division Heads who chiefly execute this growth and evaluation process. Just as a primary role of the academic administrator is to expand the capacity of the faculty, a primary role of the School Head is to expand the capacity of administrators to coach teachers. This could be the subject of an entire book. Here we offer a few brief thoughts on the subject and recommend School Heads seek out publications and resources on coaching, mentoring, leadership, and development.

'Do as I Say, Not as I Do' Doesn't Work. All too often, ISM sees administrators struggling to coach and evaluate teachers—but their own supervisor (often the School Head) does not coach and evaluate them. This sends a decidedly mixed message (i.e., "if coaching and evaluation is so important, why doesn't the Head coach and mentor me?"). In addition, it represents a huge missed opportunity to impact the life of the school by increasing the skills and confidence of the academic administrators.

For administrators and teachers to internalize the value of coaching and evaluation, the School Head must be the first to "walk the walk"—and to do so diligently. The schedule must permit adequate time each week to interact with and coach administrators. This comes in the form of being available to them as a set of compassionate and perceptive ears, actively seeking them out, and observing them as they go about their daily duties. Also, building their skills and reinforcing the value of coaching and mentoring—engaging with administrators to build a relationship and professional comfort level with them—benefits all individuals involved and the team as a whole.

To be clear, coaching and evaluating administrators include the practice that School Heads evaluate their administrators in writing annually. The excuse, "I don't need to evaluate them. We're in close contact every day—they know how I value their work," isn't any more valid than if an academic administrator used it regarding a teacher. If the School Head believes in the principles outlined in this book, he or she will take the time to evaluate academic administrators in writing.

It requires a level of knowledge and nuanced understanding. As their jobs are different, School Heads should not use the same form or template for evaluating administrators that ISM suggests using with teachers. ISM has created instruments designed specifically for evaluating School Heads, administrators, and nonteaching staff.

The differences in these instruments are based on the idea that success is different among faculty members and Division Heads. Because the skills of a high-quality teacher largely depend on discipline, pedagogy, philosophy, and intended course outcomes, a one-size-fits-all evaluation never works. This is another reason why teachers must drive their own growth. Being in a perpetual state of growth is the best "main effect" for improving all teachers' performances over time. And, because the knowledge, skills, and abilities that produce high-quality teaching is so varied, it only makes sense that the faculty member drives those goals.

For administrators, there are many leadership skills a Division Head may need to improve, and the self-directedness of their growth is also important. The most essential expectations for Division Heads are fulfilling their duties and responsibilities and the elements of the administrative agenda that stem from the school's strategic plan. Executing those agenda items serves as the primary basis for evaluating Division Heads.

The CFD Approach to Observations

Another reorientation that must occur relates to the form and function of classroom observations. The observation model for CFD differs considerably from traditional teacher observation methods, described below. Classroom observations are not to see what teachers are doing wrong or even catch them doing the "right" things. It has nothing to do with the evaluation cycle, nor is it even scheduled in a similar fashion. Rather, it is intended to assist teachers in working toward their growth goals.

Traditional Model

The traditional purpose of the classroom observation is to allow the evaluator to view the teacher in action, to make a judgment about that teacher's performance on identified areas of competence. In general, the process proceeds like this:

1. The evaluator (such as a Division Head or Department Chair) informs a faculty member that he or she will evaluate the teacher's class at a particular date and time.

2. The teacher prepares a lesson intended to impress the evaluator and asks students to be "on their best behavior" during that class.

3. The evaluator may hold a preconference meeting with the teacher to go over the checklist to be used in evaluating his or her class.

4. The evaluator observes the scheduled class, makes notes, and schedules a follow-up conversation with the teacher.

5. The evaluator and teacher meet to discuss the review.

6. The review is filed and commonly isn't referenced again (or, at least, not until next year's performance review).

Various models have been designed to execute this type of observation. The frequency and length of visits, whether the visits are announced or unannounced, the "tone" of the visit (e.g., "I'm just here to see all the things you are doing right!"), or the kinds of data collected may vary, but ultimately the purpose and result are similar. It is highly unlikely this observation will result in accountability or growth.

CFD Model

In CFD, the purpose of observations is to provide specific data and feedback to assess the success of a lesson or approach the teacher has designed in line with his or her personal goals. They typically proceed in the following ways.

1. Through the process of reaching a professional growth goal—and in collaboration with colleagues and through the "ongoing conversation"—the teacher designs a lesson or adopts an approach that might improve student learning.

2. Recognizing that feedback is helpful, the teacher invites and schedules his or her coach (or colleague, for that matter) to observe the lesson in action.

3. The coach observes the class, but mostly is interested in student behavior, so makes notes about the observable impact the lesson is having on students. The coach watches where the lesson is successful and where it might be improved. This is not to judge the teacher's competence against a standard, but to have a base of knowledge to contribute to the next conversation.

4. The coach provides any "data" (facts and observations) to the teacher.

5. At the next "ongoing conversation," the coach listens to the teacher's "postmortem" and provides support or direction when needed. The teacher and coach evaluate what was tried and the next iteration is begun.

Summary

Many books are written each year expressing new ideas, tools, and techniques for effectively coaching or mentoring employees (in general) and teachers (in particular). The healthiest faculty cultures comprise individuals who vigorously pursue continual professional development. The same applies to the healthiest administrative cultures. ISM encourages all school administrators to engage in ongoing study of ways in which they can best support their faculty. The result: Administrators make wonderful discoveries along the way, heightening their impact on the teachers they guide—and the teachers' impact on the students.

CHAPTER SIX

The Growth and Renewal Cycle

Before we discuss the elements of the growth and renewal cycle, we need to share a word or two about our choice of the terms. "Professional development" and "professional growth" are often used interchangeably, so it's important to be clear about how we are using each term. In our framework, professional development is a key component of growth and renewal, but it is not growth and renewal in and of itself.

- **Professional growth** is defined as the ongoing process of increasing skills, knowledge, capacity, and self-awareness related to one's professional role.

- **Professional renewal** is the ongoing process of engaging in reflection and recharging to remain energized about one's professional role throughout one's career.

■ **Professional development** consists of organized, finite activities designed to increase one's skills, knowledge, capacity, and self-awareness, and to energize and renew excitement about one's role. Professional development takes many forms (e.g., workshops, PLCs, webinars) and one typically engages in professional development related to a specific topic as part of the growth and renewal process.

Intersection of Evaluation and Growth

In ISM's approach to development, the only overlap between the growth and evaluation is the expectation that each faculty member is "authentically engaged in self-reflection and annual development of a growth and renewal plan." This includes developing written goals and making progress toward them. Engagement in designing and implementing improved teaching methods for oneself and one's colleagues is the norm, creating a process that is:

– personalized to each teacher;

– informed by well-defined Characteristics of Professional Excellence (see below);

– driven by that teacher's own private self-assessment; and

– supported by the coaching and collaborative relationship(s) between the faculty and administration at the school.

Elements of Growth and Renewal

A successful school focuses year after year on improving the delivery of its mission and empowering students to develop the qualities set out in its Portrait of the Graduate. (See Chapter Two.) In support of this goal, the faculty's central responsibility is to maximize student performance. The administration's central responsibility is to maximize faculty capacity.

This process helps outstanding teachers continue to grow, develop, and remain energized and engaged. Average teachers progress toward excellence, and weaker but qualified teachers improve and succeed.

The locus of control for each faculty member's growth must rest with the teachers, and they must direct the development of their own learning goals. They must see administrators as advocates for their growth and be earnest about their professional growth and renewal as an integral part of their daily experience.

Fostering a Culture of Professional Growth and Renewal

Building teachers' capacity is achieved by promoting a culture of growth, one that transforms professional development from "skill training" to an opportunity to investigate, experiment, and collaborate. This approach allows teachers to develop the tools needed to grapple with the complex and changing demands of education. It also supports the renewal aspect—teachers' ability to remain excited about their role throughout their career. These growth and renewal opportunities need to be embedded in the day-to-day structure of the school calendar, rather than set apart as "extras."

An effective model of professional growth and renewal moves away from the traditional remediation approach. Schools must evolve, providing structures and a culture that encourage and recognize the teacher as a professional. When teachers are held accountable for meeting Essential Expectations, and given latitude to invent and create practices—rather than simply implementing and adopting mandated school policies and practices—they and their students benefit.

Creating a culture of professional growth is a complex endeavor. The environment must encourage frequent conversations about, and experimentation in, the practice of teaching. Time for collaborative planning, teaching, and peer observation must be emphasized since teachers and administrators depend on one another for feedback, reflection, and support to strengthen the growth process.

Administrative Resources

A necessary component for the success of this approach to faculty development lies in the numbers—coaching and mentoring require realistic ratios of supervision. Any administrator (no matter how talented, hardworking, or insightful) can only effectively coach or mentor so many teachers. Select no more than 15 (ideally fewer)—otherwise, teacher-administrator relationships inevitably become less effective. There is simply not enough time to engage deeply with so many teachers.

When the number of teachers an administrator supervises exceeds the recommended ratio, make needed adjustments. This has several practical implications on time, money, and other resources. Remedies may include:

- **empowering Department Chairs** (or, in the middle or lower school, team leaders or grade-level coordinators) so their roles become much more actively managerial than ceremonial in nature;

- **reducing Department Chairs' teaching schedules** to free them for more active engagement with the faculty, including coaching and mentoring;

- **reducing Division Head tasks unrelated to faculty development** (such as administrative and clerical duties that can be handled by others) all them to focus their efforts on coaching and mentoring faculty members; and

- **adding administrative positions or reconfiguring reporting relationships** to achieve a more manageable supervisory ratio for administrators.

Schools that implement this process need to do so with careful planning and forethought, of course. If additional resources are required, factor these into the school's upcoming budget and strategic financial plan. Given the powerful effects of robust growth programs on faculty culture and school sustainability, the benefits should clearly outweigh the costs—but this requires patience and resilience. It may take one to three years to put the necessary resources in place. Leadership Teams need to be steadfast in seeing this process through, or the program withers from lack of attention and resources.

Characteristics of Professional Excellence

As discussed in Chapter Two, the Characteristics of Professional Excellence (CPE) are the set of unique qualities (higher-order behaviors or actions) that bring the school's mission to fulfillment in the lives of its graduates—i.e., describing "how" the mission is delivered to students. This list of aspirational, mission-aligned characteristics informs self-reflection and the creation of a growth plan. For reference, included below is the example we used in our fictional Exempli Gratia Academy (see Chapter Two), which aligned its CPE with its Portrait of the Graduate and mission statement.

Why Not Use ISM's Sample List?

ISM developed this sample CPE list as a teaching tool, so it was purposely kept generic. In contrast, each school has a unique mission, culture, and set of values, and adopting a one-size-fits-all approach won't be effective. Each school must create a set of characteristics that relates specifically to the school's mission and Portrait of the Graduate. See Example 6.1, listing Exempli Gratia Academy's Characteristics of Professional Excellence.

Example 6.1

Exempli Gratia Academy's Characteristics of Professional Excellence

The faculty of Exempli Gratia Academy commits to these characteristics as the foundation of our efforts to serve the needs of our students, colleagues, and school.

- Models lifelong learning and the willingness to take risks that serve as growth opportunities, whether they result in success or failure

- Strives to live the school mission in word and deed, bringing it to life for students, families, and the school community

- Embraces and incorporates the most current technologies and media to support learning and to prepare students for their future

- Fosters an open, inclusive learning environment that supports all students and their families through word, action, curriculum, and teaching strategies

- Enthusiastically engages in service to the school community and beyond

- Maintains a healthy work-life balance and establishes expectations that ensure balance in the lives of students and their families

---

Why Renewal?

Teaching is a giving profession (as with many service-oriented occupations). Every day, teachers are asked to give their time, talent, and energy to students, fellow teachers, parents, and to the school community. If not replenished, these energies quickly become depleted, sometimes to the point where a teacher has nothing left to give. Furthermore, in most school structures, there is little if any upward mobility within the teaching realm to provide motivation. To "move up," teachers often must become administrators, which takes the best teachers out of the classroom. (See Chapter Nine for ways to create opportunities for advancement within teaching.)

Thus, regular and ongoing renewal is absolutely required. Teachers and administrators must not lose sight of the renewal aspect of their growth programs. Without it, the program is likely to reduce over time to a perfunctory exercise, rather than one that impacts the lives of teachers and students alike. It is important to recognize that what feels like renewal varies among faculty members. Some may be energized by public recognition, additional time for reflection, time to work with other professionals, offsite fieldwork, or committee work. A key competency for coaches is to know the teachers with whom they work so well that they understand which experiences will renew and replenish.

Examples of Professional Growth and Renewal Activities

The growth activities included in any individual's plan should focus on higher-order faculty growth. Some may speak to collective as well as individual growth, thus enhancing the overall faculty culture. Keep in mind that different faculty members may experience renewal in different ways. Personalize engagement in these activities such that they re-energize and excite. Some examples include:

- **observation of colleagues' classes** within-school or at neighboring schools, as other faculty members work on new and innovative concepts;

- **faculty-led seminars** using regular faculty meetings as the setting in which an in-house panel of teachers makes presentations and leads discussion on recent studies, reading, or research;

- **teaching experiments journal,** an informal log of each new approach attempted, including the preparation involved, the outcomes, and ideas for enhancement;

- **professional publications review,** such as reviewing professional journals, blogs, articles, and discussing them with a designated colleague to draw out ideas and tools that might be useful in their classrooms;

- **brown-bag or after-school snack sessions** in which an individual offers a short presentation and leads a discussion on a special topic that he or she has studied, or has observed at another school or in another classroom;

- **professional membership,** energetically participating in professional education organizations, including attending meetings, leading workshop sessions, reading the organization's professional journal, and engaging like-minded members in various settings;

- **faculty summer reading programs,** with faculty members reporting on books that have impacted their teaching practices; and

- **action research,** with teachers examining their own practices in the classroom.

This is not a comprehensive list. Schools are wise to engage faculty members in discussions about what other kinds of growth experiences would be of interest and benefit to them.

In recommending this growth process, ISM offers one caveat—one can implement a program that is well-structured and efficient (predictability), but also lacks heart and passion (support). Conversely, one can have a program almost wholly lacking in structure, but in which reside deep passion, commitment, and energy. We suggest and encourage schools to establish a program that combines the best of each. Said differently, "It's not about the process alone—it's about the conversation" the process engenders. Thus, implementing an efficient process with which teachers and administrators comply, but do so reluctantly, or worse, resentfully, is counterproductive. Instead, the goal is a program that generates, supports, and enhances ongoing and robust conversations among teachers about teaching techniques, experiments, and all manner of growth regarding the professional vocation of teaching.

Implementing the Professional Growth and Renewal Cycle

With the definitions, purposes, and caveats outlined above firmly in mind, consider the following recommendations on implementation of a highly engaging professional growth and renewal process at your school.

1. **Establish the necessary environmental conditions (Mission-Based, Growth-Focused, Predictable and Supportive, and Student-Centered).** Leadership, including the School Head and Division Heads, should:

   – have a well-articulated mission that faculty members know by heart, and make it obvious that decisions are made with the mission in mind;

   – require professional growth as part of the necessary responsibilities of all faculty members and support it with resources (time and money);

   – insist that the school takes a student-centered approach and challenge all adult-centered decisions; and

   – emphasize a strong faculty culture, based in predictability and support, and measure it regularly.

2. **Ensure teachers know each of the Characteristics of Professional Excellence.** To engage in the growth and renewal process, each faculty member should know what it means to be a great teacher in the school. They reflect on the CPE, with feedback from previous conversations to drive their professional goals. (Again, see Chapter Two if the school is yet to develop its CPE.)

3. **Create a Growth and Renewal Design Team.** This may be the same group that developed the Characteristics of Professional Excellence, but it should include academic administrators and exemplary teachers. This team's charge is to personalize the framework outlined in this chapter to suit the school's mission and culture. The School Head supports and approves the proposed process. Team members present the proposed process to the faculty.

4. **Train Coaches.** Before implementing this system, the coaches (anyone overseeing the growth and renewal plan of a teacher) need to be trained on not only the growth and renewal process itself, but also on coaching and mentoring skills. They are then well-equipped to carry out their roles as managers and mentors. (See Chapter Five for further details and guidance.)

5. **Introducing the process to the faculty.** With the process fully formed and the leadership and coaching team trained, the growth and renewal process is ready to be introduced to the faculty. In an all-faculty meeting, the topic and model below (Figure 6.1) should be introduced by the Head or Division Head and presented by the Professional Growth and Renewal Design Team. Discuss each element of the model and provide time for feedback, questions, and feedback. The need for some minor adjustments may result.

Figure 6.1

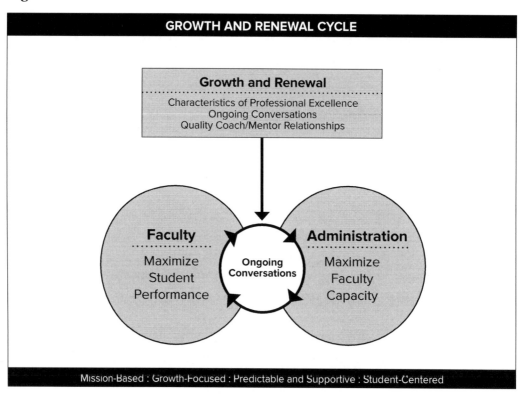

6. **Put the process into effect, teacher by teacher.** Once introduced to the faculty, put the process into effect in individual coaching meetings between coaches and teachers. Direct each teacher to spend time reflecting on the

school's CPE, processing prior feedback, and determining initial areas of professional growth that are of interest and that positively impact students. Then, in a meeting with the coach, each teacher collaborates to develop his or her initial growth plan, using the Teacher's Professional Growth and Renewal Plan Template (or a version modified by the school).

Ideally, the teacher drives the growth and renewal plan, reflecting his or her professional goals and interests. The mentor or coach's role is to listen, clarify, and be as supportive and encouraging of the teacher as possible. The mentor's job is to help make sure the plan is well-formed, measurable, and impactful. The mentor also ensures the plan is challenging but not overwhelming. Once the plan is formed and approved, the teacher is responsible for enthusiastically carrying it out. The administrator is responsible for vigorously supporting each teacher's efforts with time, attention, encouragement, and resources, as appropriate.

Some schools may decide to introduce the process gradually by inviting several teachers to "pilot" the program briefly before it becomes standard practice.

Note: While planning is needed to provide the growth plan with appropriate structure and direction, no plan should be considered set in stone. View all plans as open to revision as conditions and needs change. Don't adhere too rigidly to the original plan when circumstances may have changed. Avoid falling victim to carrying out the plan for the plan's sake, rather than carrying forth with the spirit and purpose of growth at the plan's true core.

7. **Continue the Ongoing Conversation through support, guidance, and feedback.** Hold subsequent meetings between the teacher and coach at appropriate intervals. Some goals may require only occasional meetings. Others may need several clusters of sessions to help the teacher move forward. Throughout the year, the coach provides his or her group of teachers with resources, learning opportunities, and feedback. The coach becomes an agent of each teacher's success—reiterating that "success" doesn't necessarily mean the expected outcome is attained, but rather the teacher learned and grew as a result of the effort. The administrator's availability and eagerness to give feedback, serve as a sounding board, or just provide a sympathetic ear is vital to maintaining trust in the teacher-administrator relationship.

8. **Conclude one plan and launch another.** The growth and renewal cycle is ongoing. As goals are achieved or concluded, develop new ones. Depending on the individual goal, this may happen at any time of the year.

   For example, one teacher's goal may be to increase student engagement in the classroom. One strategy may be to implement a flipped classroom approach for her first-semester elective, which finishes in December. She and her coach would meet to review the results of that strategy and begin brainstorming a new one. Another teacher may develop a new curriculum over the course of a year and a half. In concert with reflecting on the teacher's progress and growth, the teacher and administrator collaborate on drafting a growth plan for the coming academic year—and the cycle begins anew.

Several Notes About Time

The need for growth and renewal is constant and ongoing, so it can begin at any time that makes sense practically and administratively. Timing is an important consideration that the design team must address.

When allotting administrative time to guide and mentor teachers during the process, time spent varies (sometimes considerably), based on the goals selected and the experience levels, styles, communication preferences, and needs of the teacher and coach involved. It is difficult to estimate exactly how much of a coach's time the growth and renewal process requires.

ISM made reference earlier to the notion that goals aren't necessarily confined to one year. Some might require 18 months or two years to complete. As long as the teacher and coach are in ongoing conversations about the teacher's progress toward the plan's milestones, the plan length shouldn't be of concern. Continual learning and growth are the true purpose of the process.

Going back to the beginning of this book, the primary responsibility of academic administrators is building the capacity of the faculty to deliver the mission with excellence. Coaching, mentoring, and growth and renewal conversations are a primary means by which this happens, and thus is important time well-spent. We understand and sympathize with the need for schools to anticipate the burden of time. Therefore, delegate coaching and mentoring of teachers to well-trained Department Chairs or instructional coaches, with the academic administrator overseeing these coaches.

Teacher's Professional Growth and Renewal Plan Template

ISM's Professional Growth and Renewal Plan Template is shown below, again using Exempli Gratia Academy as the sample school. A blank template is included in Appendix B. As with the evaluation template, it needs to be reviewed and customized to align with and support your school's unique mission, culture, and values. As a brief overview, key elements of the template include the following.

Introduction: Overview and Instructions

Step 1: Reflecting on Mission

Step 2: Reflecting on Your School's Characteristics of Professional Excellence

Step 3: Establishing One or Two Goals

Step 4: Setting a Path to Success

Step 5: Determining the Support and Resources Needed

Step 6: Establishing Milestones and Measurements for Success

Step 7: Anticipating Student Outcomes

Step 8: Gaining Commitment

Step 9: Reflections (The Ongoing Conversation)

Introduction: Overview and Instructions

It is helpful to provide the template's users (i.e., the teacher and coach) with an overview of the professional growth and renewal process, as well as its purpose and meaning within the life of the school. Consider Example 6.2 below.

Example 6.2

Dear Faculty Member,

One of the hallmarks of Exempli Gratia Academy has always been the extraordinary energy, creativity, dedication, and passion of our faculty, which the administration strives to support in all ways possible. We understand the commitment you have to your students, and the personal and professional sacrifices you make in meeting their needs. We also understand that teachers need to renew and refresh themselves regularly to keep doing what they do with vigor and excitement.

This teacher-directed process provides a framework and support for professional development efforts. This helps you explore new ideas and gain new insights into teaching and your subject area, and doing so in a way that is meaningful, exciting, and energizing.

Directions for drafting your plan are provided on the following page. Please complete your draft and schedule an initial meeting with your coach, who will guide you throughout the year. This meeting should occur no later than September 30.

Thank you for your commitment to your students and to Exempli Gratia Academy. I offer my fullest support and encouragement as you go forward with a spirit of service and excellence.

Andrew Jones, School Head

Progressing Through Exempli Gratia Academy's Professional Growth and Renewal Process

Below is a description of the steps involved in completing the CFD Growth and Renewal Cycle. Throughout, we provide an example of one teacher's (Annette's) completed template.

Step 1: Reflecting on Mission

Note: In this step, there are two options—an active and a reflective approach. In customizing the template, the design team considers which approach (or modified version) will be most helpful.

Active option: The school invites teachers to record the school's mission statement and their own mission statements. By writing their personal missions and restating the school's mission, teachers clarify why they teach, and why they teach at this school. Understanding this may help them determine anew what resonates most strongly with them and what they want to achieve professionally—guiding them toward the growth they need and desire at this time, and that aligns with the school's mission.

Reflective option: As an alternative, the design team may choose to ask teachers to reflect on the school's mission, culture, and values—but not require them to share those reflections in writing in their growth plan. This is a thought exercise only.

Example 6.3 shows an active approach.

Example 6.3

Mission statements: Write our mission statement below—either our formal statement or in your own words. Circle or highlight the words or phrases that resonate most strongly with you. You may wish to focus on these items in this year's individual growth plan.

Exempli Gratia Academy Mission

The Academy exists to prepare students for a life of integrity, intellectual curiosity, leadership, service, and joy.

Personal and Professional Mission Statement

Compose your own mission statement. This may express why you believe you exist, your core purposes in life, the roles you play, etc.—your reason for being. A well-crafted mission statement might identify points at which your personal and professional missions intersect.

Example:

As a daughter, friend, musician, and teacher, I exist to engage with people in ways that build them up ethically, emotionally, and intellectually. As a teacher, I exist to create relationships with my students that inspire them to pursue deep, lifelong learning.

Step 2: Reflecting on Your School's Characteristics of Professional Excellence

Teachers next are encouraged to reflect on the school's defined Characteristics of Professional Excellence (CPE). Teachers may wish to focus on one or two of the characteristics that strike them most deeply. Or, they may reflect on the set of characteristics, considering the impact the entire statement may have in shaping the direction of their growth efforts this year.

Step 3: Establishing One or Two Goals

In this step, the teacher translates his or her reflections into one or two professional growth and renewal objectives for the next school year.

Limit the number of goals to two, so each goal can receive sustained attention from the teacher (and support from the coach) throughout the year. To undertake more than two goals risks the whole plan collapsing on itself, with even the most determined teachers quickly being overwhelmed by the size, scope, and volume of tasks and projects before them (while carrying out the "day job" as a teacher, of course). For this reason, many schools—especially those implementing this process for the first time—ask teachers to select only one goal.

If the school is implementing a schoolwide initiative, such as a new schedule or technology, adjusting to this initiative becomes a goal for all teachers, and counts as one of teachers' two goals. Don't add mandatory schoolwide goals on top of these. A schoolwide goal does not mean each teacher has the same professional goal. In the case of a new schedule, one teacher might need to "learn to generate engagement in an extended-length period." Another teacher might be at a different experience level with longer class periods and will, "learn to mentor students through their new 'genius hour.'" In other words, each has a goal related to the whole-school initiative, but it is customized to each faculty member's needs.

Note, the school should be aware of the demands it puts on teachers to ensure they still have room and time to choose a goal of their own. If goals are "imposed" on teachers, they may begin to believe they no longer have a hand in their own professional growth.

Important Exception

For the teacher not meeting any one of the Essential Expectations, the teacher may no longer be free to select his or her own goals. The administrator mandates area(s) of improvement. Some corrective action issues, particularly those behavioral in nature (e.g., tardiness for meetings) might allow for continuation of one of the self-directed goals. This is up to the discretion of the administrator completing the corrective action plan. When corrective action is completed, the teacher would return to a self-directed growth plan, if it was temporarily suspended.

Sample Growth Plan

Example 6.4 illustrates what goals proposed by a faculty member might look like.

Example 6.4

Annette's Growth and Renewal Plan

My Professional Growth and Renewal Goals: Briefly describe your proposed goals for this year on the lines below. You must limit your objectives to two. Please recall these objectives are designed to be higher-order behaviors that make a difference to your students and promote your own long-term professional growth and renewal. A teacher who is meeting the school's Essential Expectations is free to select two goals that inspire and drive him or her.

Goal No. 1:

Engage students outside of class in meaningful ways, such as incorporating social media as part of instruction

Goal No. 2:

Improve my ability to assess individual student progress by learning and implementing two new tools or techniques

Step 4: Setting a Path to Success

The next task for the teacher is to develop a basic outline of the steps she or he plans to take for each goal. At this stage, it is impossible to describe the actions with great precision. Rather, the intent is to develop a best-guess outline for the project—subject to developments, new information, course corrections, etc.—and chart a thoughtful course that provides direction without being unduly restrictive.

Charting a preliminary course in this way enables the teacher and coach to consider resources and timelines. Thus, if the steps require significantly more resources than are available (described in Step 5), a course correction may be needed.

(Example 6.4 continued)

Steps to Achieve My Goals

Please indicate the main steps you need to take to achieve your professional goals.

Goal No. 1:

- Attend "Social Media in Teaching" webinar
- Participate in online discussions on this topic on at least a weekly basis
- Conduct research into the various ways that social media is currently used in instruction
- Make arrangements to work with Carol Smith, who is currently using social media extensively in her grade 11 curriculum
- Visit at least two schools using social media in their upper school classrooms
- Implement at least one strategy using social media in my classroom and document results
- Prepare to report my findings at an in-service meeting

Special Issue—Socializing Knowledge: A primary intent of robust professional growth programs is the socialization of the knowledge gained—i.e., where teachers share the new knowledge they have gained with their colleagues. Sharing can take many forms, including:

- publishing an article;
- discussing findings in a Professional Learning Community (PLC) session;
- giving a presentation at the monthly faculty meeting;
- sharing findings with department colleagues over a brown-bag lunch;

- designing and displaying a poster board at the annual faculty research exhibition; or

- creating a blog with write-ups, pictures, and video snippets describing faculty research.

The teacher's newly gained knowledge must be made available for others to use, comment on, add to, and be challenged by, with the goal of affecting teacher behavior and ultimately impacting classroom practice and student achievement. Accordingly, the design team may wish to ensure that all growth plans include an aspect of socializing knowledge.

Step 5: Determining the Support and Resources Needed

The teacher is then asked to list the support and resources he or she needs to carry out the projects. This should flow from the list of steps to be taken and may include access to colleagues, journals, networks, associations, and other sources—some of which involve time, money, or both.

An example flowing from Annette's Goal No. 1 shown above might look like this.

(Example 6.4 continued)

Resources and Support Needed to Achieve My Goal

Please indicate the key resources (time, human, financial) needed to achieve your professional goals.

Goal No. 1:

- Approval and reimbursement for cost of webinar registration ($129.00)

- Reimbursement for cost of appropriate textbook (to be determined)

- Time off (up to two days) to visit schools selected to observe their use of social media in the classroom (may require substitute)

- Weekly planning period to consult with the school's IT Director and social media experts in the marketing communications department

Note: Demonstrating support by providing necessary resources is a critical issue. Particularly in the first years of the program, teachers look for signs the school is serious about this endeavor. They assess whether the school is willing to commit resources to the effort—and thus, whether this initiative is worthy of their trust and commitment—or, if this is simply the "latest fad" and soon to be forgotten. This process requires making commitments around dollars, time, relationships, etc., and the faculty will watch to see whether the school delivers on its promises. If not, the credibility of the entire process is severely diminished.

Step 6: Establishing Milestones and Measurements for Success

Now that Annette has described her two goals and resources have been determined, it is important to consider how she and the coach will know if she has successfully attained them. Accordingly, Annette is asked to forecast what success looks like with respect to the goals selected—and what milestones determine that she is progressing along the right path.

(Example 6.4 continued)

Milestones and Measures of Success: Please indicate the key milestones for keeping on track for attaining your professional goals, as well as the measures that indicate successful completion of each goal.

Goal No. 1:

- **Dec. 15**—Identify two schools using social media in the classroom and arrange to conduct visits before holiday break
- **Feb. 15**—Present research and observation findings at the in-service meeting in February
- **March 15**—Implement at least one social media element in my classroom
- **May 15**—Assess student outcomes relating to the new social media element
- **June 5**—Share outcomes of social media trial at the Faculty Showcase

---

Measures of success may take a wide variety of forms, including:

– a product (e.g., a log, diary, portfolio, video, report);

– objective accomplishment of a particular skill (e.g., a new instructional technique, mastery of a new piece of software or computer technology, a new approach to grouping students for particular activities, a new class-control approach, a revised parent education plan);

– an assessment point (e.g., a Division Head's assessment of the product and result); and

– an assessment process (e.g., a parent survey or a standardized testing event).

Failure Is an Option: Measures need not be strictly quantitative or tangible. Rather, the only requirement is that the teacher and the coach agree on what success might look like within the context of professional growth. This leads to the question of whether "success" is even required. As one school administrator put it, "Failure is an option. Stagnancy is not." Achieving a forecasted outcome may or may not indicate whether the teacher accomplished the goal. It may be the goal was, on one level, completely unsuccessful. For example, perhaps Annette could not identify any effective uses of social media in the classroom.

From a superficial level, Annette failed to achieve the goal. However, considering the goal more broadly, she may have succeeded fabulously well. She may have achieved the overarching goal of professional growth through inquiry into new topics. Further, during the research, Annette may have unexpectedly learned new techniques to use in the classroom to great effect. Or perhaps she developed a working partnership with the IT department that enhances and informs future teaching efforts in innumerable ways. The frame of reference used to define success should be carefully considered at the outset and may need to be reconsidered post hoc.

Step 7: Anticipating Student Outcomes

The final piece of the goal proposal process involves anticipating student outcomes. If the end goal of teacher professional growth is impacting student learning, then the teacher and coach must try to forecast what some of the outcomes might be.

Some outcomes might be straightforward (e.g., "student retention over drop days increases"), while others might be subtle (e.g., "my enthusiasm for my subject area is renewed, so I can communicate new passion for the topic to my students"). In either case, articulating the potential outcomes early in the program helps both teacher and coach keep the true purpose of pursuing the goal in sight throughout the project.

Step 8: Gaining Commitment

While having the teacher and coach sign the professional growth and renewal plan may seem perfunctory, the implications of this step are profound (Example 6.5). Encourage them to reflect on what they are signing off on—not from a legal perspective, but from the perspective of engendering deep commitment and accountability for both teacher and coach.

Note: Where the supervising administrator and coach are different, which may often be the case, allow for signatures by both the coach and administrator. The coach is pledging support through coaching and mentoring, and the administrator is committing to provide the necessary resources (e.g., money, time) that the coach may not have authority over.

- The teacher commits to a significant professional growth and renewal effort—embarking on a career-long conversation with his or her coach about increasing skills in ways that impact student performance, enthusiasm, and satisfaction, and ultimately support the school's success and its mission.

■ The coach (and/or supervising administrator) commits to:

– being an active success agent, cheerleader, guide, and mentor;

– providing needed resources; and

– engaging in a professionally intimate conversation with the teacher that forms the basis of their collaborative relationship.

Example 6.5

Sample Commitment Statement

An administrator's commitment to the teacher's growth and renewal is central to that teacher's success. By signing below, both parties formally accept the teacher's growth plan for this school year and agree to pursue it with the greatest professional vigor, dedication, and enthusiasm possible.

With this understanding, we agree to jointly commit to and be held accountable for this plan.

Teachers's Signature: _____ Date: _____

Administrator's Signature: _____ Date: _____

Step 9: Reflections (The Ongoing Conversation)

The power of self-reflection to help people learn and grow comes from one's own experiences. So, the final component in the professional growth and renewal process is designed to help teachers discern lessons learned from pursuing their goals (see Example 6.6). Journal space is provided to encourage teachers to reflect on the strategies they undertake, while they are involved in the process and afterward.

Example 6.6

Year-End Summary and Reflections

Ask teachers to reflect on their thoughts throughout the course of their projects (either below or in a separate document, as appropriate). Entries may be in the form of status updates; musings; or any comments that reflect their feelings, perceptions, learning, questions, and concerns throughout this process. Questions you may wish to reflect on include the following.

■ In what ways have my classes improved because of what I've learned from this project?

■ In what specific ways have I been renewed? (Or, have I been renewed?)

■ What new characteristics do I see my students developing (e.g., sense of hope, confidence, and belief in their efforts) that I can tie back to my efforts on this project?

■ What surprises, obstacles, and frustrations did I encounter during this journey?

■ What insights, ideas, or perspectives did I gain by pursuing these goals?

■ What insights, ideas, or perspectives did I gain by helping colleagues pursue their goals (that may become my goals for my next cycle)?

Required: Full Support from Colleagues

Certainly this process emphasizes the relationship between the coach and faculty member. Obviously, in the cases when the coach is not the teacher's evaluator, the teacher must be given the full support of the supervisor. But an overlooked area is the collegial relationship necessary for this process to be successful.

Teachers spend far more of their time, when not with students, with their colleagues before, during, and after, school. They work together in grade level or departmental teams. They collaborate as part of a Professional Learning Community or Critical Friends group. Most teachers look first to their colleagues for support, assistance, and a place to "bounce ideas off of." It is a more natural collaboration.

Because of the high value teachers place on collaborative relationships with their colleagues, the school should set aside time weekly for professional growth and renewal. The generic agenda for each meeting is "for teachers to talk to teachers about teaching and learning." As such, it is an ideal time to:

– share with colleagues their professional goals;

– gain feedback about innovative lesson plans;

– brainstorm with colleagues to design new approaches to enhance student learning

– share successes to socialize knowledge;

– schedule peer classroom visits;

– work on innovative joint curricular projects;

– develop interdisciplinary units or courses; and

– discuss research or books, among others.

Administrators should largely be absent from these conversations. They may "monitor" the content by requesting that groups publish a log of the conversations on a shared cloud-based document (e.g., a Google Document). The log of conversations referenced above provides coaches insights to the teachers' ideas, intentions, and upcoming plans so they have an entrée into the "ongoing conversation." Providing autonomy in this fashion signals to the faculty the responsibility of growth has genuinely been handed over to them.

Another benefit of scheduling dedicated, collegial-based professional development time is that teachers can gain insights and advance their practice through listening and contributing to the work of others. While ISM asserts two goals are the maximum amount for any one growth plan, the view into colleagues' plans expands the sphere of learning experienced by each teacher.

This time is ideally at the beginning of the school day, for an hour, and paired with a later official start time of the day. Realities in some schools require deviations from the ideal, but most barriers that are perceived to challenge a late start can be dealt with, given a little ingenuity.

Required: Full Support of the School Head

The visible and vocal support of the Head is critical to the success of the teacher growth and renewal processes. As in many other areas of school leadership, mixed messages or signs of weak executive support undermine these programs, communicating that they are potentially temporary and can be safely ignored until the school moves on to other topics of interest.

Since many schools do not currently engage in robust growth and renewal processes of the type recommended here, implementing them represents a significant organizational change effort. The implementation dynamics vary considerably based on the school's history, culture, and faculty-administration relationship. In general, the Head must clearly communicate to the faculty and administrators that:

- all teachers will develop and carry out robust professional growth and renewal plans, guided by their own thoughtful reflection and self-assessment and supported by their coach or mentor;

- the primary responsibility of academic administrators is to develop and enhance the capacity of the faculty to deliver the mission with excellence;

- appropriate resources will be provided to support growth and renewal efforts (especially in the form of time for coaches to coach and mentor faculty members, time for teachers to pursue their plans, and adequate funding to support their approved growth plans); and

– all teachers will be evaluated annually on the school's Essential Expectations (not on the extent of their growth). (See Chapter Seven.)

By sending these messages consistently in word and deed, the Head does a great deal to ensure the success of these programs—i.e., supporting the ability of the faculty to impact student performance, satisfaction, and enthusiasm in meaningful and vibrant ways.

Summary

Professional growth and renewal must become an integral part of teachers' professional lives—an Essential Expectation. This process should no longer be remediation, with the implication that teachers are not adequately doing their jobs. *Separating professional growth from the evaluation process requires a radical shift in mindset.* Furthermore, schools must champion continuous improvement while simultaneously promoting a culture of collegiality and trust—both elements are essential to the success of any initiative.

The Evaluation Cycle

Building faculty capacity is the primary responsibility of the Division Head. Extant comprehensive "evaluation" processes fail to meet this responsibility, so spending excessive time on the Evaluation Cycle or trying to use it to prescribe professional development targets for individual teachers is fruitless. However, formal periodic reviews do serve important purposes as they:

- communicate to teachers what is expected of them and on what basis they are formally evaluated;

- ensure the school that all teachers act and perform at requisite levels of professionalism;

- formally acknowledge or reward satisfactory performance;

- give the school a process by which formal corrective action can take place; and

- provide necessary legal documentation when corrective action, nonrenewal, or dismissal needs to occur.

Figure 7.1

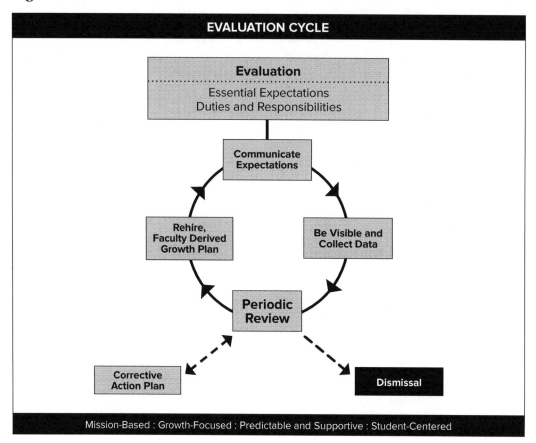

This chapter is dedicated to describing and guiding the elements of the Evaluation Cycle and providing recommendations on how periodic reviews are conducted. To these ends, the formal periodic evaluation process begins with establishing, before the beginning of the Evaluation Cycle, that only essential teacher expectations and the performance of duties and responsibilities will be the source material for the formal evaluation (see the Evaluation box in Figure 7.1). As noted in Chapter Three: Mission-Based Onboarding, both components are provided at the point of hire, and each time they are updated.

Essential Expectations

Essential Expectations (EE) are a set of non-negotiable responsibilities required of teachers for the school and classroom to operate effectively. Because the Essential Expectations are communicated during the hiring process and throughout teachers' careers with the school, it is anticipated that most teachers will meet them regularly. However, these expectations are so critical that if or when they are not being met, a formal conversation must take place immediately to address the issue.

Note that the Essential Expectations are substantially different from the school's Characteristics of Professional Excellence in that they are:

1. required as written, of all teachers from the onset of employment and as a condition for contract renewal, as opposed to characteristics of excellence toward which teachers are required to *aspire*;

2. rated on a binary "meeting" or "not meeting" scale; and

3. addressed immediately if evidence suggests a teacher is not meeting them.

Evidence that faculty members have upheld each of the Essential Expectations should be obvious through the course of the supervisor's everyday interaction with the community. They are seen in the teacher's attitude, attendance, and approach to his or her craft and in the way teachers interact with colleagues, students, and parents. Violations or evidence a teacher is not living up to the Essential Expectations will be evident in situations that arise.

The intention of making the Essential Expectations observable through common interactions within the community is to leverage the belief that (1) most teachers are meeting them, and (2) the Growth and Renewal Cycle is far more important to the quality of teaching and learning. Therefore, less time can and should be spent on the technical, legally required elements of evaluation, leaving more time for coaching and mentoring teachers toward personalized goals that directly impact the student experience in the Growth and Renewal Cycle.

ISM's List of Essential Expectations

ISM has articulated a basic set of 10 expectations, crafted for our fictional Exempli Gratia Academy (Example 7.1). This proposed list is fairly comprehensive and based on research and experience, but each school should customize the list to fit its culture. No. 10 must make the final cut because it provides the vital link between the growth and evaluation cycles. Each school should undergo a formal adoption of the expectations that involves the administration and faculty.

Example 7.1

Exempli Gratia Academy

Essential Expectations

All faculty members at Exempli Gratia Academy are expected and required to:

1. Overtly support and act in accordance with the school's mission and values.

2. Foster a safe, predictable, and supportive environment for students (see ISM's research-based principles of teaching excellence).

3. Interact with colleagues in a respectful and collegial manner that fosters a healthy faculty culture.

4. Demonstrate appropriate planning and preparation for instruction.

5. Uphold professional standards of personal presentation, punctuality, professional courtesy, and discretion.

6. Appropriately carry out specific assignments including, but not limited to, service learning, advisory programs, assigned supervision, and other areas as determined by the School Head.

7. Maintain professional credentials, as appropriate.

8. Honor the confidentiality of school, student, and family information.

9. Comply with the policies and procedures as articulated in the school's faculty and employee handbook.

10. Authentically engage in self-reflection and annual development of a growth and renewal plan aligned with the Characteristics of Professional Excellence (CPE). This includes written goals and progress toward those goals.

Developing Essential Expectations

The school's academic leadership, in concert with a representative group of exemplary faculty members, develops the Essential Expectations. This group may review ISM's sample list, the school's faculty and employee handbook, a list of the typical duties and responsibilities common to all teachers, its Purpose and Outcome Statements, and other relevant documents to inform its development of the school's Essential Expectations.

Once the group has drafted the list of Essential Expectations, we recommend that the full faculty be led through the following exercise. Create a spreadsheet workbook with an Essential Expectation on each sheet. Have three columns, one for what the expectation looks like in action, one for what it doesn't look like, and one for questions/comments. Break the faculty into interdisciplinary/interdivisional groups and ask them to generate a list of specific, observable examples each expectation in both columns. For example, what does it look like when a teacher is overtly supporting the school's mission? What would it look like for a teacher not to be overtly supporting the mission? The third column is for questions that arise or areas of disagreement. When the exercise is complete, look at the three columns to determine whether there is adequate synergy in the understanding of the expectations, and whether the expectations themselves should be revised to provide greater clarity or if further discussion/training is needed. Provide a summary of the kinds of examples teachers provided for each expectation.

You can evaluate many possible aspects. Comparing a teacher's actions against the school's particular expectations about "what's most important here" is the best way to evaluate whether a faculty member's efforts are meeting the school's needs, and by extension, the needs of students. Using these criteria consistently creates an environment of predictability (i.e., teachers know what the expectations are and see them consistently reinforced), a hallmark of a healthy faculty culture. Student test scores or other similar measures do not appropriately reflect a teacher's performance. Noticing each teacher's actions and comparing them against well-communicated and mission-aligned expectations is a fair, defensible, and effective way to judge teacher performance.

The final list of expectations must:

– be easy to detect or measure (see note below);

– constitute the necessary characteristics of professionalism for this particular school; and

– be rated on a binary scale ("meeting" or "not meeting" expectations).

Note: The teacher's success in these areas should be evident in the day-to-day life of the school, rather than in formal classroom observation. ISM reserves the observation process for the growth cycle, and our approach is different in form and tenor. The exception is when a teacher is on formal corrective action and observation is necessary to evaluate whether sufficient progress is being made.

The School Head must approve the final list of Essential Expectations. Once established, this list drives an annual cycle of review.

To reiterate and emphasize: establishing a school-specific list of nonnegotiable expectations must include a commitment to reflection and professional growth (see No. 10). It is critical to note, however, that the teacher should never be evaluated on the outcomes of the growth process. Placing an arbitrary grade on how someone grows deters risk-taking and trying new strategies. The Essential Expectations are simply whether (yes or no) the teacher authentically engages in the process.

Duties and Responsibilities

The presence of duties and responsibilities as a source for the evaluation process (see the box at the top of Figure 7.1) permits individualized aspects of a position to be included in the teacher's formal evaluation. For example, a teacher hired for a specific purpose (e.g., to also coordinate the Service Learning program) or as a Department Chair, etc., may have specific duties that would be appropriate for inclusion in his or her formal evaluation because execution of that duty constitutes an essential part of the job. Generally, these types of additional duties would be covered in Essential Expectation No. 6.

However, you may wish to document specific assignments on the list of expectations for certain roles. For example, for the Department Chairs, an additional Essential Expectation might be, "Meet with each member of the department to formalize growth goals." Note, this is NOT intended to greatly expand the list of evaluation items. Take care to include only those items that are absolutely critical to the position. Limit the number of additional duty-and-responsibility expectations to three for any individual.

ISM's Periodic Evaluation Cycle

The Comprehensive Faculty Development framework assumes and makes it possible that all teachers are reviewed at least once annually at a meeting at which the evaluator formally communicates whether the teacher is performing his or her duties and meeting the Essential Expectations. Some schools refer to this as the "annual review." ISM has chosen the more generic "periodic review" to acknowledge that if an essential expectation is not being met, meetings will be held immediately to discuss the issue at hand in an effort to correct the behavior as soon as possible, and to allow for more frequent check-ins.

Step 1: Communicate Expectations

For purposes of predictability, effectiveness, and fairness, it is important to communicate expectations clearly and consistently. The school should present them to the faculty early and often, throughout the academic year and throughout their careers at the school. In practical terms, we suggest using these approaches:

- include as part of the employment application process;
- review in back-to-school, orientation, and induction sessions;
- include as an addendum to the teacher's contract offer or renewal letter;
- discuss in direct, individual conversations with teachers throughout the school year;
- incorporate in the faculty and employee handbook; and
- discuss a different expectation during each faculty meeting throughout the year (e.g., "What do we really mean by a 'classroom atmosphere that inspires learning'?" could be a rich topic of discussion in a faculty meeting, particularly if led by teachers).

By communicating expectations regularly, the school:

- ensures the expectations become embedded in the school's culture and standard way of operating, providing a foundation in predictability;

- encourages the teacher to inculcate these expectations in his or her own mind and practice;

- helps the faculty move toward a common understanding of what the expectations look like within the school's culture; and

- solidifies its legal credibility when holding underperforming teachers accountable for these standards, should a lawsuit or other claim ever arise.

Step 2: Be Visible, Be Present, and Collect Data

We have intentionally avoided the word "observe" to eliminate the common confusion among the concepts of growth, evaluation, and "observation." We often think of observations as formal, pre-arranged visits to classrooms, after which the teacher is coached. Again, this is part of growth. To become knowledgeable about teachers' adherence to the Essential Expectations, administrators must be regularly visible to teachers in all their roles in school life. This can include:

- visits to classrooms, advisory, and athletic practices to see faculty members in the various roles they fill in the school;

- attention to interactions between teachers and students, teachers and colleagues, and teachers and parents;

- periodic viewing of assignments and tests given;

- attention to teacher contributions and behavior in faculty meetings and assemblies; and

- unstructured, informal conversations with teachers in the hallways, cafeteria, on the ball fields, in the carpool lane, etc. (Do not offer warnings or feedback in informal settings. These should always be scheduled, confidential, formal meetings.)

When observing faculty members in this manner, administrators must keep in mind the Essential Expectations described previously. These items provide the frame of reference against which observed behavior should be compared.

Psychological science research has long demonstrated the presence of others, particularly one in an evaluative capacity, impacts the performance of the person being observed. Simple, well-learned behaviors can be facilitated by the mere presence of others, whereas performance during complicated or newly learned behaviors is inhibited. Evaluators must understand this. Their mere presence can adversely impact performance, particularly when the teacher perceives he or she is being judged on the outcome. In other words, a surprise evaluative presence can introduce uncertainty to a situation when a teacher needs the fewest challenges to certainty—when trying something new.

It's essential for administrators to take notes when collecting data (Example 7.2). No one's memory is perfect. As they "walk around," it's important to note what they see and hear. These notes may include:

- the administrator's observations of the employee's performance, as well as views of the individual in the classroom and other interactions;

- observations made by others the supervisor deems credible and that serve to provide a well-rounded view of the teacher's performance;

- commendations (or complaints) shared with the administrator about the teacher; and

- reports, summaries, or other descriptions of projects or initiatives the teacher has undertaken or completed during the year—including articles in school newsletters and publications, website videos, community newspaper and magazine coverage, and the like.

A word of caution about the selection and use of examples, particularly those describing actions and events the administrator has not personally observed. Quite simply, use good judgment. Not everything reported to the administrator is accurate—and, even if it is, it is not necessarily reflective of the teacher's overall work or accomplishments during the year.

Example 7.2

Supervisor Files vs. Official Personnel Files

For purposes of organization and confidentiality, maintain notes in a secure file. The supervisor should keep a file independent of the official personnel file maintained by the school's Business Manager or Human Resources Manager. The completed, signed annual review would be part of the official personnel file, while detailed notes about interactions, pertinent emails, or other documents that support an employee's evaluation would be part of the supervisor's file. The supervisor's file is not considered an official part of the personnel file. Thus, if an employee requests a review of his or her personnel file or the school receives a valid subpoena for the employee's "personnel file," the supervisor's file would not need to be produced. However, that does not mean files are immune from subpoena—a carefully framed subpoena may include the personnel and supervisor's file. While it might be possible to get a protection order, be critical and cautious about what is included in the supervisor's file. This is particularly the case when disciplinary action was taken, as there must be documentation that supports the need for corrective action or termination. Administrators must get in the habit of filing relevant information or making notes at the time it occurs. They should consult with the school's attorney and Human Resources Manager to ensure the manner in which they are keeping notes and files appropriately protects the school's interests.

When Detours Are Necessary

If the supervisor sees that a teacher is not meeting an Essential Expectation or is negligent in a communicated duty or responsibility, immediately schedule a meeting with the teacher to discuss the issue. This meeting is not likely to be a formal periodic review (unless there already was a documented history of this teacher failing to meet expectations on the issue at hand). However, the meeting should be documented and is important in developing the formal periodic review.

During this session the supervisor must:

- avoid mixed messages by making this particular issue the only topic of conversation;
- make no attempt to soften the session with compliments or small talk;
- communicate the Essential Expectation of concern with specific, concrete examples of failure to meet it;
- approach this conversation with an open mind to listen authentically to the teacher's response, as there may well be an explanation or missing information;
- communicate the belief that the teacher can succeed and the supervisor is committed to her or his success (if this is true);
- be clear about the actions the teacher is to take and potential consequences of the failure to do so before a specific date; and
- support the teacher with suggestions and coaching.

The goals of this conversation are to:

- reaffirm the school's standards and expectations (predictability);
- further the supervisor's relationship with the teacher (supportiveness);
- expand the capacity of the teacher (as an individual) and the faculty (as a whole) to deliver the school's mission with excellence; and
- engage with the teacher in a way that inspires him or her to higher levels of performance.

If the supervisor does not believe the teacher can succeed, he or she must determine whether the assessment has been a fair one. Has the teacher ever been given useful feedback, coaching, and mentoring? Has a clear corrective-action plan been documented? If so, it may be time to discuss nonrenewal of contract. If not, the supervisor should approach the teacher from a fresh perspective with compassion, remembering that, as a leader, he or she is responsible to ensure all teachers receive the support they need to succeed.

Documentation of a conversation should include:

– the date;

– the topic of conversation; and, if applicable,

– actions to be taken, the planned date of the next meeting, and other pertinent information, such as whether this is a first, second, or third warning, and/or whether the teacher is being placed on official "corrective action" status. (See Chapter Eight for more information about corrective-action plans and conversations.)

Finally, there must be a follow-up on all conversations, to close the communication loop and ensure the teacher feels supported and knows where she or he stands. Has there been adequate progress? Is the issue still a concern? What are the next steps?

Step 3: Conduct Periodic Reviews

Having communicated expectations clearly in the form of Essential Expectations and specific responsibilities and duties, and having collected data over time, a supervisor is in a position to conduct a formal periodic review. Complete these reviews at least once annually for all teachers.

Because of the steps taken above, this should be a brief meeting with no surprises. Before each evaluation meeting, the supervisor should complete the Faculty Performance Evaluation Form (Example 7.3), having reviewed:

– notes describing examples of teachers going above and beyond the Essential Expectations;

– notes documenting meetings with teachers who have not met expectations; and

– information obtained from other sources that has been corroborated.

The school must implement any new evaluation model in a consistent and practical manner for all faculty members. The evaluation template below is designed to be clear, consistent, and user-friendly for teachers and administrators.

Each school should revise this form to reflect its personalized set of Essential Expectations, adhering to the binary "meeting" or "not meeting" expectations rating method. While adding a numerical scale, or including the rating "exceeding expectations" may be tempting, this creates a level of pseudo-objectivity and distracts from the goal of simplifying evaluation to spend more time on growth. Nonbinary scales imply a rating system, even if one doesn't really exist, that erodes the value of earning a "meeting expectations" rating. Supervisors are reluctant to give this "grade," fearing it creates complacency and teachers will hyperfocus on why they might not have exceeded expectations—everyone wants the top grade. If the supervisor wishes to identify an area in which a teacher excels, the comment box is an appropriate place.

Example 7.3

Faculty Performance Evaluation Form

Name: _____ Position:_____ Division: _____

Supervisor: _____ Supervisor Title: _____

Essential Expectations

All faculty members at Exempli Gratia Academy are expected and required to:

1. Overtly support and act in accordance with the school's mission and values.

2. Foster a safe, predictable, and supportive environment for students.

3. Interact with colleagues in a respectful and collegial manner that fosters a healthy faculty culture.

4. Demonstrate appropriate planning and preparation for instruction.

5. Uphold professional standards of personal presentation, punctuality, professional courtesy, and discretion.

6. Appropriately carry out specific assignments including, but not limited to, service learning, advisory programs, assigned supervision, and other areas as determined by the School Head.

7. Maintain professional credentials, as appropriate.

8. Honor the confidentiality of school, student, and family information.

9. Comply with the policies and procedures as articulated in the school's faculty and employee handbook.

10. Authentically engage in self-reflection and annual development of a growth and renewal plan aligned with the Characteristics of Professional Excellence (CPE). This includes written goals and progress toward those goals.

Position-Specific Expectations

1. _____

2. _____

3. _____

Rating:

❑ Meeting expectations

❑ Not meeting expectations   Date for resolution: _____

Faculty Member Signature: _____ Date: _____

Supervisor Signature: _____ Date: _____

Note: If the faculty member wishes to make additional comments, he or she may provide a written statement. This statement becomes part of the formal documentation.

Next, the supervisor schedules a meeting with each teacher for whom he or she is responsible. These meetings should take place in the supervisor's office at a time convenient for the teacher. This meeting is generally brief and comprises:

1. Review of the written evaluation form with the teacher, including the opportunity for the teacher to ask questions.

2. Acknowledgment and determination of the next steps:

   ■ For teachers who are and have been meeting expectations, the supervisor acknowledges their continuous high performance and thanks them for their contributions (being as specific as possible).

   ■ For teachers who failed to meet expectations and have since corrected the issue, the supervisor recognizes their progress and thanks them for their effort.

   ■ For teachers who failed to meet expectations and continue to do so, but are still being given an opportunity to improve, the supervisor provides dates by which correction is expected and discusses the impact on renewal of contract. (See Chapter Eight for more information about corrective-action plans and conversations.)

   ■ For teachers terminated for failure to meet expectations after receiving appropriate feedback, coaching, and support, the supervisor schedules an official termination meeting instead of an evaluation meeting. (See Chapter Eight for more information about termination processes.)

3. Suggestions from the teacher for improving the evaluation process to increase the level of predictability and support (the supervisor takes notes).

Step 4: Rehire, Reaffirm Faculty-Driven Growth Plan

The primary outcome of the evaluation is not to determine what goals the teacher has for the coming year (as in traditional approaches that comingle evaluation and growth). It's to reaffirm the teacher is in good standing and has the autonomy to continue crafting and working toward his or her own professional growth goals. If, at the periodic review, corrective action is taken, that autonomy is limited until the teacher can meet all Essential Expectations.

Also, assuming there are no school issues that will result in a reduction in force (e.g., enrollment decline), most teachers will meet the Essential Expectations and perform specific job duties as expected, and therefore, will continue to be rehired each year.

The Legal Protection Provided by Annual Written Evaluations

Acknowledge that any teacher evaluation system holds inherent legal implications. In an age of litigation and increasing federal and state regulation of employment, schools must have a substantive, regular written evaluation of each faculty member's performance.

No federal or state regulations require employers to conduct annual evaluations. However, without these, the school has little with which to protect itself against a discrimination or wrongful termination claim. An evaluation that addresses the critical elements of the job and fairly assesses the employee's performance goes a long way in helping a school prove that its employment decisions are based solely on job-related, rather than discriminatory, considerations. This can potentially save the school untold legal expenses and financial judgments, to say nothing of preventing the damage to community reputation that public lawsuits engender.

Summary

Always remember the value this process places on communication. Unless an incident occurs that warrants immediate dismissal (e.g., harm to a child, gross negligence, or other issues outlined in the school's faculty and employee handbook), there should never be a time in which a periodic review, after a series of "clean" periodic reviews, results in dismissal or failure to renew a contract. The school must adhere to a process by which coaching and warnings, when appropriate, seek to correct performance issues. While a faculty member may ultimately fail at corrective action, the trust others have in the process, the savings in recruiting and onboarding should the teacher succeed, and the legal protection prove worth the effort. This is the focus of the next chapter.

Corrective Action and Selective Retention

We have come to the final process in the Comprehensive Faculty Development Model—Corrective Action and Selective Retention. While most teachers, following a periodic review, continue on the main path of the Evaluation Cycle (being rehired and having their self-driven growth plan reaffirmed), some will not.

The Corrective Action and Selective Retention process is an alternate path, used when Essential Expectations are unmet. In other words, all faculty members go through the hiring and induction, growth and renewal, and evaluation processes. However, only a small portion of the faculty will be subject to formal corrective action at any point during their careers. Even fewer will be asked to leave the school as part of the selective retention process, particularly if the school has carefully undertaken all the processes listed above, from hiring to evaluation.

In this chapter, we explore ISM's approach to corrective action (i.e., addressing performance issues) and selective retention or dismissal (i.e., determining when a teacher can no longer continue employment with the school). This approach is consistent with keeping the school's mission, culture, and values at the center of the conversation, as they have been throughout each of the other steps in the model.

Corrective Action: Proceeding Down Dual Tracks

Most academic administrators enter the teaching profession because they are interested in supporting others in building their knowledge, skills, and abilities. This corrective-action process allows administrators to devote 95% of their coaching and mentoring efforts toward helping teachers improve in those areas.

However, in our litigious society, administrators must devote some portion of their attention to documenting their actions—to help protect the school in case a lawsuit or claim should ever arise. The reality is that being mindful of developing proper documentation is an inescapable part of contemporary management duties.

As a result, administrators need to operate on dual tracks—focusing most of their energy on enhancing teacher performance, while also being aware of the need to document actions to protect all involved. All the actions suggested in this four-step Sample Corrective-Action Policy are designed to honor these goals—focusing on performance improvement and documenting for legal protection.

A Brief Definition

It might appear the terms "corrective action" and "selective retention" are simply euphemisms. While softer, the labels "corrective action" and "selective retention" describe the intent and effect of these actions better than the more limiting and punitive terms of "warning" and "termination".

As described below, the intent and purpose of corrective action is to correct poor behavior or performance—not as punishment, but rather as performance improvement. Similarly, selective retention is just what it claims to be—a process for actively (selectively) deciding whom to retain in the school (i.e., those who are most able to deliver the mission with excellence). These terms get at the essence of what is being attempted in each case. Keeping this perspective in mind, the school gets the greatest benefit out of both processes and serves the best interests of all involved.

Elements of Effective Corrective-Action Practices

Broadly stated, mission-appropriate corrective-action practices in private schools should be:

- predictable and supportive;

- well-communicated;

- supported by policies in the faculty and employee handbook;

- well-documented;

- performance-improvement-focused rather than discipline-focused; and

- consistently (but not blindly) followed.

The first two elements have been covered extensively in this book. Predictability and support are two essential environmental conditions defining the atmosphere of every model (as well as mission-based, growth-focused, and student-centered). Predictability is established through communication, consistency in how people are treated, and the interpersonal skills of leadership. Support is felt in the coaching and mentoring approach to growth and renewal (vs. the traditional evaluation-driven method), the time and money spent in service to each teacher's growth, and in leadership's trust of faculty professionalism.

Similarly, we have emphasized the importance of communicating the Essential Expectations, as well as duties and responsibilities aligned with the Evaluation Cycle and the Characteristics of Professional Excellence in the Growth and Renewal Cycle. Communication is not merely important. Increasingly, courts are deciding against employers (including schools) whose actions appear to be in any way unfair—whether or not the actions are illegal.

Perceptions of unfairness develop when standards are not effectively and consistently presented to employees. Communicate expectations early and often, beginning with the school's first interactions with the employee (i.e., during the hiring process). For example, include several of the school's required expectations and excellence characteristics in the employment advertisement. Use the characteristics as the basis for the interview questions. In this way, the school lets employees know what is important and expected, up front and in no uncertain terms. Carry out this same communication of characteristics and expectations through each of the other CFD steps (e.g., induction, evaluation and growth, and rewards and recognition).

The other four practices—i.e., supported by policies in the faculty and employee handbook, well-documented, performance improvement-focused, and consistently followed—also apply to the rest of the CFD Model elements, but take on significant importance during corrective-action and dismissal processes.

- **Supported by Policies in the Faculty and Employee Handbook:** One of the Essential Expectations is to "comply with the policies and procedures as articulated in the school's faculty and employee handbook." Any corrective-action and selective-retention process must be supported by a well-crafted faculty and employee handbook. A multi-warning process when corrective action is initiated is included below. However, there may be particular issues or violation of handbook policies that would initiate immediate dismissal. To protect the school:

  – review the current faculty and employee handbook and policies (e.g., attendance, dress code, insubordination, boundary issues, religious affiliations if applicable);

  – include the faculty Essential Expectations in the handbook;

  – consider outlining potential deviations from a multi-warning system for certain offenses (particularly those that involve harm to children, harassment or discriminatory behavior, violence, or misrepresentation of credentials); and

  – obtain legal assistance to review the school's policies to be sure they comply with federal and state laws. (See also Appendix A.)

- **Performance Improvement-Focused Rather Than Discipline-Focused:** Consistent with the purpose and spirit of the CFD Model, orient corrective-action efforts toward improving performance (i.e., building up employees so they can meet the school's high standards) rather than punishment-oriented (i.e., focusing on catching employees doing things wrong so they can be disciplined). This provides:

  – consistency with a growth-focused faculty culture;

  – alignment with the school's mission, culture, and values; and

  – fair treatment and actions that support faculty members, which not only sustain healthy employee morale and the overall faculty-administration relationship, but also provide significant legal protection, should the situation devolve into legal claims.

- **Well-Documented:** Courts expect termination decisions to be well-documented. Incomplete, shoddy, or ill-considered documentation significantly damages a school's ability to defend itself against any claims or suits brought by terminated employees. To this end, the school's records must contain a clear statement of:

– the standards communicated to the teacher;

– the steps taken to support the teacher in achieving satisfactory performance;

– the stated consequences for failing to attain required standards; and

– should termination result, the manner in which those standards were applied.

■ **Consistently (But Not Blindly) Followed:** When dealing with lawsuits and claims, it greatly aids a school's defense if it can show that, in similar situations, employees were treated in the same way. This is not meant to imply, however, the school needs to defer to precedent without room for judgment. While corrective-action policies are intended to provide predictability (consistency) of actions taken, it is impossible to create policies that address all possible situations that may occur. In any given situation, the Head must act in the school's best interests—even if this differs from what was done in seemingly similar situations in the past or must address a never-before-encountered situation. The School Head in particular (and the Leadership Team in general) is entrusted to manage the school using sound judgment, which necessarily implies accounting for subtleties and nuances that serve to distinguish situations. To this end, avoid creating a corrective-action policy that has "written itself into a corner." That is to say, policies should serve the school, not the other way around.

Sample Corrective-Action Process

Corrective-action processes generally include several steps, each one leading progressively to more serious consequences (giving the process its other name, "progressive discipline"). The goal is to help the teacher return to performance levels that "meet expectations"—in the school's Essential Expectations and in any other evaluated duties and responsibilities—as soon as possible. If this does not occur, the situation, and the risk of termination, becomes increasingly more serious. Note again there are some issues that warrant deviation from the four-step process outlined below.

1. **First Warning:** When it is observed or comes to the attention of management that a faculty member is not meeting expectations, the supervisor should immediately schedule a meeting with the teacher.

This typically does not need to be a full periodic review (i.e., rating on all elements of the Essential Expectations). The issue should be the only item on the agenda. Document the meeting to support movement to a second stage, if necessary. Present the evidence of the below-expectation performance and clearly communicate the expected behavior. Establish, communicate, and present in writing a plan for remedial (corrective) action and a date for a review. If the teacher does not correct the issue to the level required, the administrator ordinarily moves the process to its second stage.

Note: First warning does not necessarily mean first notification. Many scenarios do not warrant a warning. Initial infractions may not warrant an official warning. A "concerned inquiry" and coaching conversation might be the appropriate first step. For example, if a teacher misses a faculty meeting, the supervisor might simply state the fact, show concern for the teacher, ask for an explanation, and reinforce expected behavior. Of course, the supervisor should still document the conversation. Then, if the teacher misses another meeting, a warning would be appropriate.

2. **Second Warning:** If the first warning is not effective in changing the behavior or improving performance to satisfactory levels, then issue a second warning, typically in concert with a full periodic evaluation. This is similar in nature and substance to the first warning, only with the explicit proviso that the situation is now more serious and the teacher is at greater risk of termination if the issue is not corrected. Suspend the teacher's ability to self-determine professional development goals until the performance on the specific Essential Expectation or responsibility is remedied.

3. **Third Warning:** If the behavior or performance issue continues, the process advances to the third or final warning stage. As with each prior step, prepare a written warning document and provide the employee with enough time and support to rectify the performance or behavior issues involved. In accord with the progressive discipline concept, tell the teacher the situation is now serious—he or she is at the final step before termination is considered.

4. **Termination or Nonrenewal:** If the first three steps are unsuccessful, a decision may be made to proceed to termination. This could be immediate (in the case of an insubordination, negligence, or performance issue) or result in nonrenewal at the term's end (the more usual case). This is the aforementioned selective-retention decision. Specific considerations around communicating and carrying out this action are discussed in further detail later in this chapter.

Common Questions About the Corrective-Action Process

In its work with schools, ISM fields many questions from administrators about the corrective-action process. Below are three of the most common.

■ **Who is the supervisor—and what authority does he or she have?**
In some schools, it may be unclear exactly who the "supervisor" is—and who is invested with the authority to issue a warning or make a termination decision. Is it the Department Chair or the Division Head—or only the Head?

Most commonly, consider the Department Chair or Division Head the direct supervisor, with the power to issue warnings and recommend termination. But only the Head is empowered to make the termination decision. Regardless of who communicates the decision, the teacher must be made aware the person with the appropriate authority has made the decision and supports and enforces the actions being taken.

■ **When does the situation move from "coaching" to "warning"?**
This is a major step, and a difficult one. Administrators have to grapple with determining when an issue crosses the line. It is largely a matter of experience in knowing when the situation is serious enough to require a formal warning rather than a friendly coaching or counseling session. The line varies based on the circumstances. In general, though, issue a warning when, after repeated coaching sessions:

– the situation does not seem to be improving; and

– moving to a more serious level of interaction is the best means for holding the teacher accountable for improving his or her performance.

In the coaching and mentoring discussion, the School Head must sometimes serve as the "coach of coaches." This is one such instance. Inexperienced academic administrators often require considerable coaching around these matters so they can discern when moving to formal corrective action is the necessary and appropriate step to take. School Heads need to be prepared to spend significant time with junior administrators, guiding them through the emotionally and intellectually draining efforts of managing a teacher through a corrective-action process.

■ **How much time do I need to give them to improve?** The time frame must correspond to the nature of the issue. If the issue is behavioral (e.g., not turning in grades on time, lateness), it is reasonable to expect immediate improvement. For more nuanced performance issues—

fostering a predictable and supportive environment, for example—it is not realistic for skills to improve overnight. A time frame of a month, or a quarter, or the remainder of the academic year might be appropriate. In all cases, clearly state the deadline when providing the warning—to provide predictability (knowing what is expected).

When the Four-Step Process Shouldn't Be Used

Returning to the theme that all processes should work for the school and not against its interests—i.e., not restrict it from taking necessary action—it is important to understand corrective action in context. One aim of the process is to provide a predictable framework of action and response for administrators and teachers. It is not, however, designed to be used at all times and in all situations—especially those involving student, teacher, or community safety.

Egregious, dangerous, harmful, or risky behavior (e.g., theft, violence, inappropriate conduct with students and parents, and the like) requires immediate action. Deal with these situations promptly and decisively (though still fairly and prudently). If a teacher has placed a child in grave physical danger because of careless behavior or dereliction of duty, do not feel compelled to progress through multiple warning steps before terminating the teacher. Often, after investigating the facts, such behavior would prompt a final warning—or immediate termination.

Use good judgment to decide when to apply the corrective-action process, and when the situation warrants other, more urgent action.

Customizing the Process

The four-step process shown above is a sample model. Each school should reflect on its own culture and values, then modify the process accordingly.

One common question regarding customizing the process involves when to put the warning in writing. In many schools, the first warning is positioned as a verbal warning—to convey the idea that "the situation is serious, but not yet serious enough for us to put it in writing." Whether the process starts with a verbal or written warning, all concerned must understand that they have now entered a formal process with particular consequences. That a verbal warning has occurred should be documented with the date it took place.

Putting the Process in Writing

Publish some description of the corrective-action process in the faculty and employee handbook—for meeting the predictable and well-communicated goals noted. The school may choose to describe the process in brief, general terms, or in more detail. Example 8.1 shows both types of descriptions.

Example 8.1

Sample School Corrective-Action Policy (Brief)

Any employee who violates the school's policies, guidelines, rules, and/or standards of conduct or performance may be subject to corrective action up to and including termination. Depending on the severity or frequency of the violation, corrective action may involve a short series of warnings, becoming increasingly more serious in nature. The school expressly reserves the right to determine the severity of the problem and the preferred method of proceeding in each individual case, based on the facts and circumstances involved.

Corrective-Action Policy (Detailed)

Exempli Gratia Academy encourages our employees to develop and perform to their fullest potential at all times. When an employee's performance or conduct does not meet established standards, we do not look to punish but rather to support the employee quickly, effectively, and eagerly in correcting the behavior or improving his or her performance. The school has developed the following general procedure for addressing most behavior or performance issues.

Please note: While the school intends to address most common performance issues in the manner described in this policy, employees should be aware the school maintains all its rights under the employment relationship (whether those rights are at-will rights or contractual rights, as may apply). The school does not restrict itself from altering its approach to corrective action as circumstances warrant, at the School Head's sole discretion.

Two common exceptions to the corrective-action process are:

- misconduct or other serious behavioral issues, especially circumstances involving risk to students or other employees, will ordinarily be addressed promptly and firmly outside the process described in this policy; and

- with employees who are new to the school, the school and the employee may quickly determine there is a misalignment between the employee's skills and interests and the school's needs in the position. In these cases, plans to resolve this misalignment ordinarily may be handled promptly and separately from the process shown in this policy.

Step One: First Warning

When a performance or conduct issue arises and informal attempts to resolve the issue or correct the performance are not successful, the employee will be provided with a written warning and a conversation will occur between the supervisor and the employee.

Step Two: Second Warning

If the performance or conduct issue is not rectified in the manner or time period provided in the first warning, the employee may receive a second warning. The supervisor and employee will again meet to review the matter and establish a mandatory action plan to help restore the performance to satisfactory levels. The employee should be aware that ongoing performance issues may place him or her at more serious risk for termination or nonrenewal of contract, as may apply.

Step Three: Final Warning

If the employee's performance does not meet standards within the agreed-on timeframe of the second warning, the supervisor may provide a final written warning to the employee. The employee should be aware that further performance issues place him or her at grave risk of termination or nonrenewal of contract.

Step Four: Termination or Nonrenewal of Contract

If the employee's conduct and performance do not improve as required, the school may choose to terminate the individual's employment, or not renew the employee's contract for the following school year.

Note that both versions of the policy expressly state the school's right to alter the process in its sole judgment, based on the facts involved. This is a crucial provision to prevent the school from unduly restricting its ability to act as needed.

Documenting Poor Performance and/or Conduct

When implementing the corrective-action process, the administrator enters a realm of action in which documentation is crucial for protecting the school. When preparing to carry out corrective action, two key questions arise.

- What do I document?
- How do I document it?

The answers are that, regardless of the step in the process, essentially the same information is written down and communicated to the teacher. That is, every conversation (warning meeting) and document in the process should contain the following information.

1. Situation or actions observed (what happened). Explain the problematic behavior or performance as specifically as possible—striving to state the facts and eliminate emotion from the situation.

For example, the supervisor might state: "In the past two months, we have spoken on four occasions about your communications with parents—including your timeliness when returning emails and phone calls and your tone and demeanor when speaking with parents. We've discussed our 24-hour callback policy written in our faculty and employee handbook. But I continue to observe that you do not meet it (as you acknowledged in our conversation last week), waiting over a week to return parent contacts. Also, multiple parents have provided feedback as to your negative tone in the communications, while you have described your calls as 'highly confrontational.'"

This explicit, factual description of the situation is different—and much better positioned to protect the school in any ensuing litigation—from an emotional, nonspecific statement such as, "I always have to bail you out of conflicts with parents."

2. Applicable performance or behavior standards (what should have happened). Wherever possible, the warning should make reference to established standards. For example, "The school's policies require all teachers to return emails and telephone calls to parents within 24 hours, and with the proper tone communicating warmth, professionalism, and caring."

Add a statement of why this is important (i.e., describing the negative impact of the action). For example: "Failure to be an effective communicator with parents is mission-inappropriate. Our mission clearly promises an attentive and nurturing community. It also negatively impacts the school's reputation and may ultimately impact retention of students."

3. Required action and time frame (what needs to happen and when it needs to happen). Continuing with our example, the school might indicate that: "Effective immediately, parent communication must correspond with school standards as to tone, demeanor, and responsiveness. Return all emails and telephone calls within 24 hours."

4. Support available (how the school can help). This is where the school indicates what, if any, assistance is available to the teacher. For example: "To assist you, we have hired a communications coach who will meet with you for two hours after school each Tuesday for the next month to work with you on communication skills. We have also provided two stickers with '24 hours!' printed on them for your computer and office phone (these reminders will be made available to all faculty members)." This aspect of the warning goes directly to supportiveness.

Note that now the locus of control of the faculty member's goals for growth has shifted from self-directed to being directed by the corrective-action process. It will not be possible or appropriate for the school to provide support in all situations. In the example above, the school might not have the resources to provide extensive communications training to the teacher. However, where possible, making school resources available demonstrates a sense of fairness and supportiveness—qualities consistent with private-school culture and that also help enhance the school's credibility should legal claims ever arise.

5. Corrective-action step (where we are in the process). Clarify what step in the process is involved. For example, "This is considered a first warning, which is the first of three potential steps in our corrective-action process before a termination or nonrenewal decision." A brief summary of the corrective-action process may be provided here, as well as a statement of the steps that have been taken. Even in stating this, however, the school should include the disclaimer that it reserves the right to condense or alter the process if circumstances warrant.

6. Consequences of failure (what might happen next). Communicate the consequences for not meeting the required performance or behavior standards in the specified time frame. For example, "Failure to meet the specified performance standards may result in further corrective action, such as issuance of a second warning or further corrective action." Again, this goes directly to the question of clarity (predictability) and reinforces the seriousness of the issue.

Conducting the Corrective-Action Meeting

Approach a corrective-action meeting as a formal coaching and counseling session. The goal is to engender the employee's recognition of the issue and gain his or her commitment to altering performance or behavior to meet school standards. That said, while communicating a serious message from the school, this is also an opportunity for dialogue to explore the employee's ideas for self-correcting the behavior. When used in this way, the meeting has the greatest chance for gaining the teacher's buy-in and commitment to change. Base the planning for and conducting of the corrective-action meeting on the following principles.

- Appropriate time and setting: To communicate the seriousness of the discussion, always hold the meeting in a private setting without outside distractions. For example, it should take place in the supervisor's office or a private room rather than while walking down the hall, sitting in the faculty lounge, or standing on the sidelines watching the school's soccer team play a match. Informal settings dramatically reduce the impact of the meeting as well as the legal protection provided, sending mixed messages about the seriousness and urgency of the issue.

■ Nonemotional discussion of the issue: While by their nature performance discussions may become personal and emotional, the supervisor must endeavor to stick to the facts. Emotional statements like, "You're always so ____" or "You're never____" may sound to the teacher like personal attacks rather than substantive, objective judgments. If the administrator communicates the messages in this tone or style, he or she risks having the process perceived as personality-driven rather than job performance-related.

■ Clear communication of the current stage of the process: For most teachers, it is a shocking and deeply personal issue for their performance or behavior to be questioned—even if this occurs in the most respectful, nonemotional way possible. For this reason, it is particularly important to communicate calmly and clearly that this is a formal corrective-action process—and to specify the stage in the process, as well.

As obvious as it may sound, it is nevertheless vital to say the words, "This is a formal warning" in the discussion. Otherwise, it is easy (and understandable) for the employee to perceive the conversation may be simply a "friendly chat" akin to all the other coaching discussions with his or her supervisor in the past. This diminishes the clarity and impact that a warning is intended to have.

■ Teacher's commitment in changing behavior: The school's goal is to correct behavior, not to punish it. This is much more likely to occur if the employee understands the seriousness of the situation and commits to righting the ship. Employee buy-in can be gained by seeking employees' input into the action plan they need to carry out to make the behavior or performance changes a reality.

Ultimately, the supervisor is always in control. Nothing the employee says alters the warning being issued. However, being receptive to the employee's ideas on how to correct the situation, the supervisor gains the employee's engagement. This also provides legal protection (i.e., courts ordinarily recognize the fairness and credibility of processes in which the employee was involved in establishing action plans and milestones). Example 8.2 shows a fictional scenario.

Example 8.2

VIGNETTE: A 'Drive-By' Warning

It is axiomatic that we can learn from good and bad practice. This vignette illustrates generally poor (albeit common) practice with regard to providing corrective action to teachers who are not meeting the school's established standards. See how many actions you can identify that violate the principles described in this chapter—and then be sure not to repeat these same errors in your own corrective-action practices.

Setup: Sue Williams, Upper Division Head, has been putting off having a verbal warning discussion with Bill Jergensen, American history teacher in the upper school. Sue bumps into Bill as she's leaving her office for a meeting in the lower school building. It is lunchtime and the corridors are crowded and noisy as students bustle past them on their way to the cafeteria.

Note: You may wish to read the "dialogue" column in full, then loop back to the commentaries for notes and perspectives.

Sue: Oh, Bill. Hi—how's it going?

Bill: Great, Sue. How about you?

Sue: Not bad. Listen, I'm glad I ran into you. Do you have a minute?

Bill: Sure thing.

Corrective-action discussions should always be private, prescheduled meetings, conducted in a manner reflecting the seriousness of the event. They should never be off-the-cuff, spur-of-the-moment conversations—and never held in public, noisy, and distracting settings.

Sue: Great. There's been something that I've been meaning to talk with you about. But, before I forget, I just wanted to thank you for the fantastic job that you did last week leading your government class on the overnight trip to the state capital. I hear the kids really got a lot out of it.

Bill: My pleasure. I really enjoyed this year's group. Who knows, we may even have an aspiring politician or two in the class.

Sue: Now that would really be something. Say, I have to run to a meeting in a minute, but there was one other thing.

Present warnings as single-topic meetings. They are different from performance evaluations, which attempt to include strong and weak performance points from the full academic year. For purposes of clarity, focus a warning meeting only on the immediate issue.

Bill: Sure. What's up?

Sue: I was just wondering, was there a problem getting papers back to students in your classes earlier in the fall? I've gotten some calls and all ... [voice trails off]

Sue isn't presenting the concern clearly—i.e., is the concern that she's "gotten some calls," or is the concern that Bill's action didn't meet standards? Clearly state the latter here.

Bill: Yeah, I got a little behind at the time. Molly's parents were both ill, so she had to go take care of them while I held down the fort at home with the girls. Plus, my favorite team made it to the World Series this year, as you know—so that distracted me for most of October, I have to admit. Anyway, I just got a little backed up on grading, that's all.

As the bell rings signaling the start of the next class, the conversation continues.

Sue: Oh, sure. I see. Well, it's just that it seems like I've gotten these calls every once in a while. It's nothing much, I'm sure. You know, it's just that I have to be responsive.

If the behavior or performance is serious enough to warrant a warning, never diminish with phrases like "It's nothing much." That statement presents a mixed message that is in stark contrast with a formal warning.

Bill: [defensively] What do you mean, "these calls"?

Sue: [nervously] No big deal, really. You know how parents are these days—all upset if their little darling didn't get their A+ paper back as quickly as expected.

Bill: [offended] You don't think there's a problem, do you? I mean, I've been here eight years, Sue, and I've never been questioned before by anyone.

Sue: Questioned? No—nothing like that. Just see what you can do, OK?

Bill: [suspiciously] Is there anything else that you haven't told me about that I should know?

Sue: [trying to sound casual] Well, now that you mention it, a few of the parents have complained that you didn't respond to their calls right away, either. It might have all been around that same time, though.

Again, Sue misses an opportunity to emphasize the importance of standards being met. She diminishes the issue again, and also fails to state the expectation clearly (such as grading papers within "x" days or responding to phone calls within "y" hours).

Bill: Sue, you said it yourself. You know how some of these people are. They act like we're the hired help or something—like we have to drop everything to speak with them immediately, no matter what else is going on.

Sue: [reassuringly] Listen, I'm sure that it will be fine. Just a little blip on the radar screen. I just had to mention it, that's all. Hey, sorry—I've got to run. Good job again on the trip.

Sue lessens the seriousness of the warning with every part of this statement.

As Sue departs down the hall for her meeting, Bill wonders to himself:

Bill: [confused, angry] What was that all about? "All these calls."

What did she mean by that? Did I just get reprimanded for something that wasn't my fault? I mean, after eight years, what's with all the questions? Don't they know how much I do for this school? Good luck trying to find someone to replace everything I do—and at this pay level, too. They don't know how good they have it with me here. I know I don't like it one bit, that's for sure.

While there are no formal, legal standards for what constitutes a "warning," it would be difficult for a reasonable person to conclude that Sue formally warned Bill. This would certainly be questioned if the situation devolves further and a second warning is necessary—to which Bill would likely respond, "Where was the first warning?"

At the same time Sue is thinking to herself:

Sue: [relieved] All right, then—check that one off the list. It didn't go too badly, really. What was all the worrying for? He seemed to take it pretty well. I mean, when you're as established as Bill is, it's got to be pretty shocking to get a verbal warning. I didn't want to do it—but I've got to show that I'm on top of things. At least it's done with. I'm sure he got the message. Now, when I get back to my office, I just have to remember to write this down. Our new Business Manager is whispering in the Head's ear and she's making us record everything these days. Great—more paperwork.

And quite frankly, given the setup and history of Bill, this should have been a "coaching session," not a warning!

The Question of Witnesses

Should a witness be present during warning or termination discussions? As a general matter, do not have a third party (such as another administrator) present in the meeting for witness purposes.

From a human resources perspective, this does not add much weight to the school's case (i.e., having two people corroborate the school's words and actions), even though attorneys often recommend this practice. Instead, the witness's presence immediately sends the employee the message that he or she is not trusted, or the school feels threatened or vulnerable (all of which are counterproductive to correcting the behavior or performance in question).

Include a third party, however, when that person contributes information or ideas pertinent to the problem-solving focus of the discussion. For example, if the Head meets with an employee, he or she may bring in the employee's Department Chair to brainstorm professional growth opportunities to aid the employee in resolving the performance issue. Any third party included must, of course, be in a position appropriate to being involved in the performance discussion (such as a Department Chair, Division Head, Dean of Faculty, or the like). Otherwise this person's presence may be considered random, confusing, or unhelpful by the employee.

Coaching the Coaches: Preparing Administrators for Corrective-Action Meetings

The School Head recognizes that often nothing is more daunting to inexperienced administrators than the prospect of conducting a corrective-action meeting. This is particularly true if the administrator is considerably younger or less experienced than the teacher involved, or if the teacher is considered to be unusually difficult or aggressive. Regardless of the individuals or circumstances involved, it is often productive for the School Head to help junior administrators anticipate and practice responding to issues through role plays and other discussions.

The School Head, academic administrator, and possibly the Human Resources professional, might meet in advance to:

- discuss the written warning document;
- prepare for the corrective-action meeting by planning the agenda;
- chart the order in which to discuss issues; and
- identify any potential objections to the points being raised. Anticipating objections allows the administrator to practice in a safe setting so he or she can respond more clearly and confidently when the meeting occurs.

This approach not only builds the administrator's confidence in dealing with performance issues, it also enhances the coaching or mentoring relationship between the Head and the administrator. Such skill- and confidence-building pays significant dividends, including greater legal protection for the school and greater capacity for administrators to address thorny performance issues in the future.

When All Is Said and Done: Time to Part Ways

School administrators tend to be hopeful individuals by nature, commonly drawn into educational administration by the belief they can make a difference in the lives of individuals—first students and then adults (faculty and staff). It is this core conviction that makes administrators constantly strive to help poorly performing faculty members address those issues.

Sometimes, though, the situation reaches a point where the school has done all it can to support the teacher. When this occurs, the inevitable conclusion is that the school must end the employment relationship with the teacher. Again, this is why this process is termed "selective retention"—the school is actively selecting whom it chooses to retain and not retain.

The remainder of this chapter discusses issues related to selective retention (termination), including how to know when it is necessary, how to carry it out, and how to document the actions taken.

Knowing When Enough Is Enough

School Heads often ask, "How do I know when enough is enough? How do I know when the warning process should end and it is time to terminate the teacher?" In one sense, the answer is, "You'll know when you get there ... and not a minute before." While this may sound glib and unhelpful, the knowing when that time has come is as much an emotional reckoning for the administrator as it is a checklist of items to consult. School administrators who sincerely try to give teachers every opportunity to succeed (such as through a credible corrective-action process) usually do what is necessary to cover the school legally well before they come to peace with their decision internally. When technical and emotional readiness have been achieved, the administrator is ready to move toward termination.

Administrators can double-check their own emotional readiness and the appropriateness of the decision by consulting the following list of actions and events. It is time to proceed to termination when the following conditions are true.

- The school clearly communicated expectations to the teacher on multiple occasions.
- When the teacher struggled, the school provided resources to support him or her—e.g., coaching, remedial instruction, peer support, and the like.

- When the teacher continued to struggle, the school provided additional resources, guidance, or support.

- This continued until the administrator involved:
  - couldn't identify any more resources or support the school could reasonably provide; and/or
  - saw clearly the teacher was simply not aligned with the school's core purposes, culture, or values, and that this was unlikely to change; and/or
  - perceived that students were being poorly served (or were being harmed) by the faculty member's efforts; and/or
  - observed the individual's poor fit, toxicity, or other behavior was clearly damaging the school's faculty culture.

Types of Terminations

Terminations in private schools are usually one of two varieties:

- *nonrenewal:* the contract is not renewed at the end of its term and the faculty member is not invited back for the following school year; or

- *midyear termination:* the faculty member's behavior and performance is so problematic that he or she must be terminated before the end of the contract.

Due to the significant disruption that midyear teacher terminations cause with students (interrupting their learning flow) and teachers (disrupting the faculty culture), they are relatively rare. Nonrenewal actions—i.e., deciding not to offer the teacher a contract for the following year—are considerably more common.

Termination Provisions in Contracts

In most contracts—including teacher contracts—one of the most important provisions concerns how to end the contract. Teacher contracts should clearly specify the conditions under which the contract may be terminated by either party.

Two particular issues arise in contract termination clauses.

- **Permissible reasons for termination.** Many contracts specify that midyear (i.e., mid-contract) termination can only occur "for cause." Cause is then spelled out as a short list of particularly egregious behaviors or actions, such as being derelict in duties, placing a student in harm's way, and the like. If the school terminates the employee mid-contract for a reason not on the list, the termination would be invalid and the school would be placed in breach of contract.

- **Final pay.** Sometimes contracts specify a "notice period" (such as 30 days) for which the employee is paid in the event of a valid termination. In this case, it is clear what the employee is owed. However, what if the contract is silent on the issue of termination payouts? In this case, a court would likely rule that the employee be paid for the remaining time in the contract, absent any mitigating information to the contrary. This is because a contract is for a set term (e.g., 10 months), and the assumption is that the employee is due pay for the entire contract, as agreed.

Schools should carefully review their contract language with their employment attorney, ensuring that it is clear what is being committed to in the contract, especially regarding reasons for termination and final pay.

Employment At-Will and Employment Contracts

Most U.S. states operate under the doctrine of employment at-will. This means that the employer and the employee are free to end the employment relationship at any time for any reason, or for no reason at all. However, this doesn't protect most schools because, in schools that use employment contracts with teachers, employment at-will does not apply.

By offering the teacher a contract, the school acknowledges the contract governs the terms and conditions of employment, rather than the employment at-will doctrine governing the employment relationship. Thus, rather than the school being free to end a teacher's employment at any time for any reason, it can only terminate the teacher for reasons and under conditions permitted by the contract that it has entered into voluntarily with the teacher.

Fairness and Nondiscrimination Always Apply

To a large extent, examining the distinction between at-will and contract employment is a matter of concern primarily for the school's attorney—not its academic administrators. Administrators must keep in mind that certain principles apply in all terminations, regardless of at-will or contract status.

Understanding and acting on these principles help protect the school in any lawsuits or claims that arise.

- **Fairness:** Courts seek to determine whether the employee had appropriate notice and was given a fair chance to rectify performance issues (such as through the progressive steps of a corrective-action process).
- **Compliance:** Another key issue a court reviews is whether the actions taken comply with the relevant policies or legal documents that preside (i.e., the school's policies and procedures or the teacher contract).

- **Nondiscrimination:** Both elements above contribute to the court's judgment about whether discrimination against the employee may have occurred—or whether the school based its actions on job-related skills, experience, and performance demonstrated by the employee (which is nondiscriminatory and thus safe and legal).

Conducting the Termination Meeting

Once a termination decision is made, the School Head or Division Head must use care and discretion in preparing for and carrying out the meeting with the teacher. These key principles support a successful process.

- **One-way communication.** A termination meeting is one instance in which dialogue is not sought—this is designed to be a one-way communication. The purpose is to inform the employee about the decision and the reasons behind it. The teacher, however, may push back with questions, explanations, and requests, and may become emotional. Engaging in long dialogues about such matters can serve to escalate conflict in the present or become fodder for future lawsuits. However, one should not be abrupt or cold when trying to limit unnecessary dialogue either—as you may also escalate the emotionality that will inevitably be present by refusing to answer any questions. Balancing being clear, concise, and empathetic is key. See the vignette below for guidelines on how (and how not) to direct the meeting back to its intended purpose.

- **A firm attitude.** The Head should not schedule the meeting if he or she is at all uncertain or wavering in a decision. Regardless of the employee's response to the termination news, the Head needs to be committed to carrying out the decision in full.

  If the faculty member hears or perceives mixed messages—such as, "I wanted to keep you on, but the Board won't agree"—the opportunity for legal claims rises substantially. The employee is now aware of differences of opinion, and a divide-and-conquer legal strategy becomes possible. The plaintiff's attorney can claim the split of opinion reveals the termination wasn't based on objective, irrefutable facts, but rather on the personal and perhaps discriminatory animus of one of the parties.

- **Scripted remarks.** Ad-libbing the reasons for termination is risky, so the Head must carefully prepare the key points to be communicated during the meeting. For example, a termination meeting agenda ordinarily includes:

  – why the meeting is being held;

  – why this action (termination or nonrenewal) is being taken;

- what has led up to this action (review of previous warnings, dates, and results);

- what this action means in the short term—i.e., whether the teacher is being asked to finish out the semester, and under what conditions;

- what documents are being provided—such as a termination letter, final paycheck, and COBRA information (see below); and

- how the return of keys, laptops, equipment, etc. will be handled.

- ▪ **Documentation.** The Head needs to work closely with the school's employment attorney on this point, as requirements may vary by state. Documentation in typical terminations includes:

  - termination letter (briefly recounting the process that led up to the termination and providing details around final pay, when continuation of benefits [COBRA] information will be sent, etc.); and

  - final paycheck, if required to be provided immediately under state law or under the terms of the contract.

- ▪ **Logistics.** For immediate terminations (i.e., when the date is the employee's last day with the school), consult security and IT personnel (in confidence and as appropriate) before the termination meeting to make necessary arrangements to protect the school and its systems (e.g., computer logins, keys).

- ▪ **Preparation for the emotional component.** Last, but definitely not least, is the need to prepare for the emotions that inevitably come up during termination meetings. Heads often face terminating a teacher who is a friend, a fellow member of a church or civic group, a neighbor, a parent, etc. Terminations in private schools carry more emotion than in many other organizations. Role-playing "what-if's" and rehearsing the meeting's content may be desirable, if an appropriate individual is available to serve as a sounding board and confidante.

The following role-play (Example 8.3) shows the emotion involved in termination meetings.

Example 8.3

VIGNETTE: Managing Through an Emotional Nonrenewal Meeting
Termination discussions are never easy, even for the most skilled and experienced school leaders, because of the emotions and economic and career realities that come to the fore. It is important for Heads to anticipate and practice dealing with their emotions in advance—such as in role-play or other practice discussions with

an appropriate sounding board. The vignette below is designed to bring to life some of the emotions and conflicting issues and influences that are often present in termination meetings.

Note: While this Head does a generally good job of handling the discussion, she stumbles at a few points and implements a few solutions that are strongly recommended against, as noted in the commentary segments.

Set-up: Mary Jane Young, the School Head of a K–8 private school, is meeting with Tom Cunningham, physical education instructor. In his fourth year of employment, Tom is affable and congenial. He participates wholeheartedly in faculty events and activities. He has two children in the school and receives substantial financial assistance, which enables him to afford the excellent education his children are receiving. Many of the students adore Tom and take private tennis and golf lessons from him on breaks and during the summer.

Mary Jane has asked to meet with Tom at 4 p.m. today. It is the Friday before spring break.

Note: You may wish to read the "dialogue" in full, then loop back to the "commentary" segments for notes and perspectives on the dialogue.

Tom: Hi, Mary Jane. I got a note that you wanted to see me. Is this a good time?

Mary Jane: Yes, Tom. Thanks for coming. Please have a seat. So how are things going today?

Tom: Terrific! Thanks for asking. We started our softball module this week, which is always the kids' favorite. Plus, I'm helping out at the middle school's tennis tournament this weekend. How are things going with you?

Mary Jane: Well, to be candid, it has been a tough week. I've been meeting with the admin team all week looking at our staffing for next year, and we've had to make some tough decisions about personnel—which is always the hardest part of my job.

Mary Jane does a good job of getting to the point respectfully without digressing too far into excessive pleasantries (which would be common, because of nervousness).

Tom: I can imagine. They say, "it's lonely at the top," you know!

Mary Jane: Yes. Well, that is what I wanted to talk to you about, actually.

Tom: [uncertain] OK.

Mary Jane: I need to talk with you about your contract situation.

Tom: Hmmmm.

Mary Jane: Tom, over the past three years, we've spoken on many occasions about your lack of progress on your professional goals. I've tried to help you—with Linda, your Division Head—to support you through recommending workshops, engaging in our PLC groups, and suggesting some great books that would help you grow to be a better phys ed teacher. However, we have now gone three years without your having reached a single goal, and this year you failed to specify your professional goals in writing. After serious consideration, Tom, we just don't see the situation improving. Therefore, we've decided not to renew your contract for next year.

Tom: Wow. I can't believe you're saying this! I just had no idea the situation was this serious. Why didn't you say something to me sooner—or at all, for that matter?

Given the serious impact of a termination as a "professional death," as it were, it is not uncommon for employees to react with emotions akin to dealing with death and dying (denial, anger, etc.).

Mary Jane: We did, Tom. Reviewing my notes, I see that you and Linda had conversations about this on October 20th, November 18th, and January 7th, as well as the warning memo that we gave you in February.

Tom: Sure, we talked a few times—and I admit that Linda has been pushing me to come up with written goals. But I thought that I had time to really dive into them once the school year ended and I wasn't so busy.

Mary Jane: But Tom, these same conversations have been going on for the past three years—almost as long as you've been with the school.

Mary Jane properly communicates the prior steps in the corrective-action process that have led to the termination decision.

Tom: You know how much I care about this school and how much my girls love it here. How are they going to feel when I take them home today and tell them they can't come to school here anymore because their daddy's been fired?

Mary Jane: I appreciate your commitment to the school, Tom. You've been a role model in many ways. But we have to make decisions based on what is best for our students.

Tom: Can't you give me just one more chance, Mary Jane? I don't know what I'll do without this job. I mean—we haven't told anyone yet, but we just found out that my wife, Jeannie, is expecting again. One of the girls is just starting with the orthodontist. We bought a new car recently, because our old one died. I don't know how we're going to make it.

Tom's statement indicates there may not have been clarity around the seriousness of the warnings. Or, it may be that everything was done and communicated properly, but he could not process the impact because of denial issues.

Mary Jane: Tom, I understand that this news means you have to find a new way forward. But please know the school does care about you. That's one of the reasons I felt the decision needed to be made now. The last thing I wanted to do was to string you along for another year believing that everything was OK when it wasn't.

Tom: It just doesn't seem fair. I mean, whenever Linda and I talked, it was always pretty informal. I think one of the times you mentioned was a two-minute discussion on the sideline at the soccer game. Nothing that led me to think, "Hey, this is serious."

Tom begins his emotional appeal here. Expect this, especially when the facts of the performance issue are not on the employee's side.

Mary Jane: I'm sorry if there were any mixed messages, Tom. But I believe that we gave you every opportunity to succeed.

Tom: Isn't there anyone else I can talk to about this? What about Jerry Richards, the Board Chair. We really hit it off at last year's golf outing. If I could convince him to give me another chance, would that get you off the hook—so you didn't have to do this now?

It wouldn't be unusual for a teacher to attempt to bargain his or her way out of the termination by calling in the influence of a third party.

While the Head is ultimately responsible for employment decisions, he or she must have the implicit and explicit support of the Board in all termination matters. Otherwise a breach can be opened that is dangerous to the school on several levels.

Mary Jane: I'm sorry, Tom, but my decision is final. I've discussed each of the staffing moves that we're making with Jerry, and he supports me fully on this. Now, I need to explain—

Tom: It's just not fair, Mary Jane. You know, Linda—she's a piece of work sometimes. One day she's my friend and one day—well, she's always had it out for me, ever since I started here. I know that she wanted to hire a female phys ed teacher instead of me. She didn't like me breaking up the all-girl party in the lower school. I bet that's it.

I really should probably see my lawyer about that. It all makes sense now. I always knew there was something I couldn't trust about her. She's so two-faced—gosh, I've always disliked her.

Tom's broad claim of potential gender discrimination should be reported to the school's attorney when debriefing on the results of the meeting. However, if the school's facts are in order and if it has considered all pertinent information leading to the termination decision, new claims ordinarily shouldn't derail the process at this point (i.e., during the termination meeting).

Mary Jane: Tom, this isn't about Linda or about anything else other than your performance and whether you are a fit with the position. It was a hard decision, but we had to make it, for the good of the students.

Tom: For "the good of the students"? What, do you think my teaching was harming them or something?

Mary Jane: No, Tom—that's not what I mean at all. Please listen to me. Our decision is made and we need to put this behind us now and move forward. We've prepared a few documents to provide you with the information that you need. The first one—

Mary Jane appropriately redirects the discussion from personality and interpersonal issues back to the facts of the termination decision, properly placing the needs of the students first.

Tom: I can't believe it. I got fired. I got fired. How am I ever going to explain this to Jeannie and the kids? How am I going to tell them they have to switch schools and that we may have to move, all because their dad is a loser who couldn't even keep his job? This is a nightmare, just a nightmare.

Mary Jane: Tom, please don't say those things about yourself. They are not true. You're a very good person and great with kids—just not in a classroom, necessarily. Your true talents may lie elsewhere. Please know that we're going to do everything we can to help you land on your feet. I know that this is an emotional time—I understand that. Maybe you want to take a moment to compose yourself?

Termination discussions are commonly nonlinear because of the teacher's emotions and reactions. Use some time and patience to accommodate the inherent emotions, but not to extremes. Ultimately, the conversation needs to go forward—allowing, of course, for appropriate attending to emotions.

Tom: What? I mean, no, thanks, Mary Jane. That won't be necessary. I'll be fine. It's just that it's now hitting me like a ton of bricks—the reality of it, that as of June

15th I'll be unemployed. I know that you've always been good to me, Mary Jane. You've looked out for me. And while it's hard to understand, I believe that you're looking out for me now, even though I don't deserve it. I appreciate it, I really do.

Mary Jane: OK, then, Tom. If we can continue—let me explain the documents that we've prepared for you. Is that OK?

Again, Mary Jane calmly turns away Tom's attempt to divert the discussion and returns to the idea the conversation must move forward.

Tom: Yes, of course.

Mary Jane: The first document, for our files, is a letter informing you that we won't be renewing your contract for next year, for the reasons that we've discussed. It also explains that you will be paid through the end of June, and we are asking you to fulfill your job duties for the rest of the term. The second is a letter of reference. It says that you were "laid off because of budget cuts." We felt that this would help you in finding your next job.

The first document, stating the reasons for the termination, is absolutely appropriate. It is helpful to lay out the pay-related consequences, too, as Mary Jane has done.

Tom: Am I really being laid off? Is that true? Does that mean I might get rehired— maybe I won't have to leave after all?

Mary Jane: I don't want to give you any false hopes, Tom. It doesn't mean that. Your contract is not being renewed. It isn't a lay-off and you won't be rehired. Do you understand that?

Tom: Oh, OK. [dejected] I understand. But what am I going to tell people, the other teachers? I don't know how I'll be able to face them these next three months.

Mary Jane: What you choose to tell people is up to you, of course. Officially, the school's files will simply indicate that your contract was not renewed—nothing more, nothing less. And the reference letter states that it was because of budget cuts. If anyone asks me about it, I will tell them, as I always do, that we do not comment on personnel issues, as a matter of policy.

The second document is where Mary Jane makes her first significant mistake. Schools should never create or distribute documents that misrepresent the facts. Tom is not being "laid off because of budget cuts." This greatly blurs the message and creates documents that could potentially put the school at risk of losing a lawsuit in the name of trying to protect Tom's feelings. False documentation is never recommended in any circumstance.

Tom: OK, thank you. I appreciate that. I'm going to have to think about what to say. I need to talk with Jeannie.

Mary Jane: Between now and the end of the school year, the Business Office will provide you with—

Tom: I'm sorry, Mary Jane. I'm just thinking now about applying for jobs. Can you help me with that—pass along a good word for me with people you know, other Heads, that is? Can I put you down as a reference on an application?

Mary Jane: The letter of reference is supposed to serve that purpose, Tom. Officially, it is our policy not to provide verbal references for any employee. However, given the circumstances, I promise you that I will do whatever I can to help.

Communicating the reason that a teacher is leaving is always a delicate matter. Mary Jane does a good job of leaving this to Tom's discretion as a personal courtesy—except of course, for the false documentation involved.

It is not uncommon or necessarily inappropriate for the school to negotiate a letter of reference in cases such as this. However, it is important for the school to avoid saying or implying anything in writing about the employee's performance or service that it doesn't believe and can't document (either positive or negative).

Tom: Will I be eligible for unemployment? I mean, if I don't end up with a job in another school, it may take me awhile to land on my feet. I just need to know if I can plan on getting unemployment—the $350 a week, or whatever it is, will sure make a big difference.

Mary Jane: I can't say for sure, Tom. That is up to the Unemployment Department. All I can tell you is that we'll tell them you were laid off because of budget cuts. They make their determination. The school is not involved at all.

Defer all discussions of unemployment benefits, pointing the employee toward the appropriate government agency. To enter into this discussion suggests the school has control over the matter, which it does not. Mary Jane does a good job of communicating this (except, of course, for the false reason of termination).

Tom: Right. I understand.

Mary Jane: Now, I realize that this has been difficult news for you to hear, Tom. I know that you will probably have more questions as time goes on. So, once we're back from break, please feel free to make an appointment and we'll discuss any other questions that you have. Meanwhile, the Business Office will be in touch with you to talk about benefits, your final paycheck, and those sorts of things.

> **Tom:** I know that Jeannie will have lots of questions. Is it OK if I call you at home during the break?
>
> **Mary Jane:** It would probably be best, Tom, for us to handle things in the office once we're back from break. [Pause] However, if it is an emergency, yes, I'll be home this week and you are welcome to call—if it is urgent.
>
> **Tom:** Thanks, Mary Jane. I really appreciate that. I just still can't believe it.

Special Topic: Separation Agreements and General Releases

Occasionally, there may be unique circumstances related to terminating a faculty member that require special considerations above and beyond the ordinary process described above. This may include situations which the school has not managed well (such as a long-time teacher with performance issues that haven't been actively addressed until now) or in which the facts are not fully in its favor (such as the teacher who is clearly not competent but to whom a supervisor has also made inappropriate remarks about gender or ethnicity).

These cases should not arise often. However, when they do, handle them with appropriate humility and discretion. Acknowledge that, because of a blurring of facts and circumstances, the school has some complicity in the matter and must resolve the situation in a way that protects itself. In these cases, the Head may wish to consider use of a Separation Agreement and General Release.

Note: Consult with legal counsel before putting such an arrangement into place. This agreement essentially offers the employee an "exchange." The school provides the teacher with additional compensation not otherwise owed him or her. In exchange, the employee provides the school with a release from liability— i.e., agreeing that he or she will not file a lawsuit for actions that occurred during his or her employment (such as for discrimination or wrongful termination).

Consider two key components when offering a separation agreement.

1. The compensation (called "consideration" in legal terms) must be significant enough for the employee to waive his or her right to file a claim (e.g., two or more months of pay is probably the minimum acceptable figure; two weeks' pay is generally deemed insufficient).

2. Legal time frames must be observed (most particularly for employees over the age of 40). The employee must be given up to 21 (or more) days to consider the written agreement when it is presented, and then up to seven days to revoke his or her consent once the agreement is signed.

Again, the circumstances that warrant this agreement should be few and far between. However, when it applies, it should be an option that is reviewed by the Head and the school's employment attorney.

Coda: A Risk That Must Be Taken

Any school (or other employer) can be sued at any time for any reason. Administrators have long ago come to grips with this reality—otherwise the school couldn't open its doors to administrators, teachers, staff members, and students every morning. That being said, terminating an employee is a particularly risky venture in today's litigious environment.

The paradox here is that this risky action is also necessary for the school's protection—i.e., to protect the students, teachers, and school culture—when it comes to removing a teacher who is underperforming, misaligned with the school's culture and values, or both. Therefore, the action must be taken where warranted—but taken in a way that is most likely to protect and support the school in all realms.

To determine whether terminations are being handled in a way that protects the school and its highest purposes, review the school's actions against the following questions.

- Has the school reflected seriously on its mission, culture, and values, and identified specific Characteristics of Professional Excellence and Essential Expectations that describe the core behaviors and attitudes required in its teachers?

- Have these characteristics and expectations been communicated consistently, starting from the school's recruitment advertising and job posting notices?

- Have these characteristics and expectations been used as the basis for interviewing qualified candidates?

- Have these characteristics and expectations been used as the criteria for selecting candidates for hire?

- Have these characteristics and expectations been emphasized and explained during the school's induction process?

- Have these same characteristics and expectations been established as key criteria in the school's performance evaluation and professional growth and renewal programs?

■ Have these characteristics and expectations served as the key criteria and standards on which progressive corrective action was initiated for underperforming teachers?

Of course, nothing can provide 100% protection to a school, especially when terminations are involved. However, when the school has made the above the foundation of its interactions with the faculty, its administrators can feel confident of having done the best possible job of protecting the school and its students and teachers.

Compensation

Now that methods for hiring and inducting teachers, creating a growth-focused professional culture, and separating and simplifying the evaluation process have been addressed, the next issue to grapple with is faculty compensation. This chapter briefly touches on traditional (nonperformance-based) approaches, quickly moving to the central focus: providing compensation that recognizes and rewards excellence, aligns with the school's mission, and supports a healthy faculty culture. Note that while this chapter refers primarily to salary as compensation, the school and employees must recognize the true value of the compensation package (e.g., salary, health benefits, retirement contributions, paid time off, anniversary bonus).

Traditional Compensation Structures in Schools

For decades, private schools have used one of two primary methods for compensating faculty members:

– salary grids, basing teacher pay on years of experience and educational degrees; or

– individually negotiated contracts, basing teacher pay on direct negotiation between the teacher and the School Head. (Legally speaking, the School Head [CEO] and CFO are usually the two people authorized to enter into contracts. However, employment contracts, while signed [authorized] by either the Head or CFO, are often negotiated by any number of people, e.g., HR Director, Division Director.)

Both methods have their positive and negative points. Whichever compensation method is used, it is essential to include a statement of confidentiality regarding salary in employee contracts.

Salary Grids

Also known as the ladder system, this structure is based on the approach used by most public schools. A teacher's starting salary is determined by years of credited teaching experience, as well as the highest degree earned. Consider the sample below.

Table 9.1

A Common Salary Grid			
Years	**Bachelor's**	**Master's**	**Doctorate**
0, 1, 2	$52,854	$58,270	$63,669
3	$52,872	$58,291	$63,691
4	$52,890	$58,312	$63,715
5	$53,857	$59,402	$65,926
—	—	—	—
15	$65,190	$73,375	$79,537
25+	$73,879	$82,199	$90,494

Note: This chart is for illustration purposes only. The figures shown should not be considered benchmarks or recommendations in any regard.

While the benefits to this system include predictability, transparency, a sense of "equality," and ease of administration, the downsides outweigh the benefits. The negatives of this system are that:

- it implicitly assumes (inaccurately) there is a significant relationship between years of experience and degrees, and teacher performance (i.e., "We should pay teachers with more experience and advanced degrees more than less-experienced or less-degreed teachers. They perform better and have a greater impact on students"). In general, research has concluded that after five years, "experience" levels off as a single factor on students' performance, and there is little to no evidence that advanced degrees impact student achievement; and

- there are no pay-related consequences for mediocre or poor performance (since pay is solely based on experience and degree). This can lead to the unfortunate situation in which salary raises for high-performing teachers are restrained because of the need to pay long-serving but mediocre-performing teachers ever-increasing salaries over time.

The Individual Negotiation Model

This model, popular with many private schools, does not necessarily assume that a teacher has a contract in the legal sense. This compensation model assumes:

- an individual, likely the School Head, assumes responsibility of assigning compensation to every individual faculty member;

- when a teacher is first hired, his or her pay rate is determined in the negotiation process with the School Head;

- compensation rates are adjusted annually based on the budget;

- while there are not fixed steps or increases, the most frequent adjustments assign an increase to all faculty based on the Board's approved budget— usually cost-of-living (COLA); and

- while this system does not preclude negotiation in future years, it does assume that most faculty will receive similar annual percentage raises.

The benefits of the individual negotiation model are that it:

- responds to the labor market. If competitive conditions require the school to make higher salary offers to secure desirable candidates, the Head is not restrained from doing so by a fixed grid specifying what the offer must be. For example, perhaps the school is hiring a chemistry or physics teacher, and labor market conditions and competition dictate that starting salaries be x-percent higher than for World Language or English teachers. The Head can craft a market-competitive offer for the candidate; and

– provides flexibility to recognize and reward excellent performers with higher-than-usual year-to-year increases. For example, when determining next year's salary offer, the Head can consider an individual's performance and competitive pressures, such as whether the school risks losing this person to a competitor.

The downsides of this approach are that it is:

– not predictable for the school. The school cannot completely determine its salary budget in advance because it does not know how market pressures or a faculty member's leverage may force larger-than-usual salary offers in a particular year. Similarly, a school may have a high faculty turnover rate in a particular year, and this may not be known when budgeting, adding uncertainty to the process;

– completely nontransparent. Faculty members do not know the basis on which their peers are paid and potentially see it as arbitrary. If teachers compare their salaries (violating the recommended confidentiality clause), and there are discrepancies (i.e., one teacher makes significantly more than another without obvious reason), it can damage the collegial nature of the faculty culture by creating a sense of unfairness;

– unpredictable for the teacher. A teacher cannot predict his or her salary from year to year, as it depends on economic and labor market conditions, and the teacher's ability to be an effective negotiator; and

– open to claims of favoritism and discrimination, because there is no fixed basis on which salaries are set. In the example above, the Head could make a higher-than-usual starting salary offer to an incoming science teacher because of market and competitive pressures. Such an offer is completely legal and reasonable. However, if there are additional factors—such as the teacher is a friend of the Head's family, is the only male on the science faculty, and would make more than the veteran Science Department Chair (who is female)—a claim of favoritism and discrimination could easily be made. While the claim might or might not succeed in court, the school leaves itself open to costly litigation or settlement talks, to say nothing of the attendant negative publicity.

Note: ISM research has revealed a consistent gap between the salaries of male and female teachers in private schools—with males consistently being paid 5%–15%

more than females across every slice of data. Individually negotiated contracts can exacerbate this problem. Also, if such a situation is present in a school with individually negotiated contracts, the school has little to protect itself if sued by female teachers claiming gender discrimination.

Simple Merit Pay or Pay for Performance

The risks and downsides noted for salary grid and individual negotiation models, combined with burgeoning societal changes, have elevated merit pay as a third model used in private schools. While merit pay (also known as "pay for performance") had previously been anathema for most private schools, conditions since the early 1990s have prompted school leaders to reconsider the topic. These conditions and pressures include:

- Board members increasingly calling for pay-for-performance models similar to those they are familiar with from their "day jobs" in for-profit organizations;

- increasingly competitive pressure forcing schools to focus intently on ensuring high performance from all faculty members. This makes them less financially able to "carry" mediocre or poorly performing teachers until they choose to retire of their own accord; and

- changes in the perspectives, attitudes, and expectations of newer teachers about their ability (and need) to influence their compensation, particularly their ability to grow salary in ways that aren't dependent on "putting in their time and paying their dues" over many years.

The Expectations of Generation X and Millennial Teachers

Examining the last factor in more detail, ISM's experience is that it is largely (but not exclusively) the younger and less experienced teachers who are most concerned with increasing their pay aggressively. From a generational perspective, these teachers reflect different motivations than their predecessors. School leaders continually report that Gen X and Millennial faculty members:

- want a defined way to grow their salaries;

- want to be recognized for the value they add to the school;

- are willing and able to negotiate their salaries; and

- will leave a school when their salaries fail to match their perceived personal and professional investments (of time, energy, commitment, etc.).

The Simple Merit Pay System

In the past, many schools have used a simple merit pay system, a basic framework that provides the school with salary increase ranges based on the past year's performance. The simple merit frameworks require the use of the formal periodic evaluation to "grade" teachers along each of the dimensions (e.g., "At-risk," "Weak," "Strong," and "Exemplary"). Because of this connection to evaluation, simple merit pay is not compatible with the Comprehensive Faculty Development Model. The same problems (i.e., lack of discernment between poor, good, and great teachers; inadequate evaluation metrics; lack of time spent on faculty development) that underlie traditional evaluation systems would erode trust in this merit process.

Evaluation of teachers, as defined in Chapter Seven, is solely based on meeting or not meeting Essential Expectations. Thus, any teacher employed by the school is either satisfactorily meeting the expectations or is in a corrective action process that leads to the teacher's improvement or termination. Since all teachers are accountable to the same high expectations as determined in the evaluation system, evaluation will not distinguish one teacher from another in terms of merit.

Never connect pay to teachers' growth plans. As explained in Chapter Six, successful growth requires risk-taking, failure, and recovery. Evaluation of or tying consequences (such as compensation) to growth, stunts growth and defeats the system's purpose. When growth is confused with or combined with evaluation or pay, this damages faculty culture and trust in administration.

Broadbanding

Instead of the simple merit pay system described above, any school wishing to reward and recognize exemplary teachers and provide them with a defined way to grow their salaries, should adopt the broadbanding option. Broadbanding does not tie salary to growth and evaluation, but rather to clearly defined objective achievements.

Note: For broadbanding to succeed, a predictable and supportive environment needs to exist in which the faculty trusts the school's administration. As explained in Chapters Six and Seven, an effective growth and evaluation system is essential in fostering a healthy faculty culture. Teachers must perceive the growth and evaluation system to be fair, useful, and meaningful. The system must have been in place and operating smoothly for a minimum of two years before it can be universally regarded and trusted. Schools overeager to institute broadbanding with a new growth and evaluation system risk confusion between the two and concern that compensation ties somehow to evaluation and growth, gravely damaging the credibility of both initiatives.

In its essence, broadbanding is a strategy that outlines a salary path without guaranteeing a predetermined salary. Rather than seeing annual increases as discrete events based on that year's performance evaluation, broadbanding considers multiple years of performance—in the form of accomplishments that take several years or more to achieve. Establish bands of qualifications to help teachers and administrators identify increasingly impactful levels of contribution to the life of the school. Faculty members must meet specific criteria to advance their salaries (i.e., to earn annual increases and to move upward from band to band) and remain employed by the school.

The broadband structure is designed to achieve several objectives.

- It gives the school maximum flexibility to recruit and retain high-performing faculty members by allowing the Head to reward outstanding performance with differentiated starting salaries and pay raises. It enables the teacher to have maximum influence over his or her salary growth by allowing for annual increases based on meeting objective criteria outlined in each band. This also provides the opportunity for additional leaps in salary when moving to a higher band or achievement within that band.

- It communicates predictability (e.g., "Here is what we are expecting of you within each band—and here is what your salary will be like when you meet those criteria") and supportiveness (e.g., "We are dedicated to helping you be successful in meeting your goals").

- It aids the Business Office in planning the salary line of the operating budget by providing a reasonably predictable (though more expensive) structure and framework around salary increases.

Similar to our comments about merit pay, ISM sees several marketing realities driving private schools to broadbanding structures, including:

- increased competition for the best teachers (in every discipline);
- competition with the corporate sector for teachers with particular kinds of training (such as in technology, science, and math);
- the need to provide differentiated compensation to attract the above categories;
- the desire to compensate exemplary faculty members so they aren't compelled to go into administration simply to improve their financial position;

    – the desire to provide leadership opportunities for exemplary faculty members without obligating them to leave the classroom for administration; and

    – the desire to enable teachers to make lifestyle choices (impacting compensation choices) as they move from one life stage to another. For example, a teacher may choose to downshift from the rigorous expectations of a higher band to the slightly less taxing requirements of a lower one, to spend more time with the family.

Forming a Design Team

The first step when implementing broadbanding is to appoint a committee to drive this effort. At several points in this book, we have recommended appointing teams of faculty members to create necessary structures (e.g., the design teams created to customize the school's Characteristics of Professional Excellence and Essential Expectations). Appointing mission-appropriate, exemplary members follows the same suggestions as for the other noted teams and committees.

If the administration develops the bands alone, without use of a committee that includes teachers, the Head and her deputies must work harder to communicate the system's purposes and foster ownership among faculty members. If, however, a faculty committee develops the bands, there will ordinarily be more up-front investment, given the credibility of the team members. Teachers and leadership should collaborate in some form on developing the banding and criteria to ensure, to the extent possible, proper construction and faculty ownership. Carry this out through either a back-and-forth process of a faculty committee creating drafts and leadership providing feedback or a single mixed group of faculty and leadership.

It is essential that those teachers and administrators charged with developing the bands are well versed in this new approach so the bands conform to the necessary structure and reflect real changes in student impact. This is an important point, as research in the public school system has shown that compensation bands are often poorly constructed. If done poorly, no matter how much teacher investment is achieved, broadbanding eventually fails as levels are too difficult to manage, too easy to progress through, or too irrelevant to student performance.

Establishing Band Criteria

Regardless of its membership, the Broadbanding Design Team's charge would be to establish a series of progressive bands that define the criteria for band membership. Each level contains relevant markers that describe increasing levels of faculty achievement, responsibility, or evidence of student impact.

While this ultimately translates to money, money is not the team's concern or purview—dollars will be attached to the bands later by the Business Manager and School Head. Rather, the team's focus is solely on developing the bands and the associated criteria for moving up from one band to another.

Note: Create a four-band system. Fewer bands become too restrictive and more levels make it difficult to discern between teachers at each band.

As with prior design teams, this group may take six to eight weeks (or longer) to complete its work. And, just as with the other teams, it is the quality of the work that counts, not its brevity. Accordingly, the Head or another academic administrator should be regularly involved with the committee to offer encouragement and support, and to provide any resources or guidance necessary. The result of the team's work might look something like the following example from our fictional Exempli Gratia Academy.

Criteria for Moving From Band to Band

In reviewing the Exempli Gratia Academy sample broadband (Example 9.1), it is important to note the goals in Band A are fairly easy to achieve, emphasizing professional development and participation in school activities. This helps teachers early in their careers to focus on classroom basics, while placing increasing responsibility on veterans. A teacher should clearly understand expectations at Band A, and what he or she must do to progress to Band B, and beyond that to Band C and Band D.

Bear in mind the following elements when developing band movement criteria.

- Except for the entry-level band (i.e., Band A), require teachers to remain at a given band a minimum of three or more years. This is to ensure that skills and experiences gained at each level are embedded in the teacher's makeup, rather than demonstrated on a short-term basis solely for purposes of progressing up the band structure.

- As a teacher moves up the bands, his or her increased contributions to the school should be evident.

- Graduate degrees should not be required to move to higher bands— advanced degrees do not necessarily correlate with teaching excellence. However, many schools have traditionally encouraged teachers to gain advanced degrees as a means of career progression or to market to the community a high percentage of the faculty with advanced degrees.

Example 9.1

Sample Banding Structure
Exempli Gratia Academy Broadband Faculty Compensation Structure

A dedicated team of teachers and administrators has collaborated on the following structure representing performance levels sought and expected by the school of its faculty, and through which teachers are recognized and rewarded.

Note: To be considered for band advancement, teachers must be consistently meeting Essential Expectations, a requirement for continued employment at the school.

Band A

Teachers with 0–5 years of total teaching experience (e.g., a novice educator entering the field and the Exempli Gratia Academy culture) are placed in this band. To progress to Band B, the teacher must complete at least four of the following:

- attend a beginning teacher institute

- complete an approved learning experience on classroom management

- participate in a professional education association or group

- self-assess his or her teaching using *Teaching Excellence: A Research-Based Workbook for Teachers* (also available from ISM) and use the results to drive professional growth

- shadow a teaching mentor for one day

- maintain a reflective journal of professional readings and experiences

- present to the faculty at large the results of a professional growth initiative. Include in the presentation the objective, lesson design, summary of feedback from at least three student-impact-based observations, adjustments made, and anticipated impact on students.

Decision point: Following three years at Exempli Gratia Academy, a teacher must qualify as either a Band B or higher, with his or her supervisor's endorsement, or the teacher will be released from employment.

Band B

A teacher with three or more years of total teaching experience, a committed educator. The goal at this level is to:

- provide professional growth experiences that promote a teacher's further commitment to the school; and

- optimize his or her potential to impact positively the lives of the students.

To progress to Band C, the teacher must successfully complete the criteria in Band B and at least three of the following:

- join and participate in a group that provides professional collaboration (e.g., Critical Friends, Professional Learning Community—PLC)

- participate in a national or regional educational conference

- attend a conference or seminar addressing technology in the classroom

- attend a conference or seminar addressing cognitive science applied to the classroom

- maintain a reflective journal of professional readings or experiences

- complete at least one of the following:

- serve actively on a faculty committee addressing a student-related issue

- conduct an action research study and report the results to an in-service faculty session

- present to the faculty at large the results of a professional growth initiative. Include in the presentation the objective, lesson design, summary of feedback from at least three student-impact-based observations, adjustments made, and anticipated impact on students.

Decision point: When the teacher is ready to progress to Band C (after at least three years in Band B) based on the criteria, he or she must submit a self-evaluation and band progression report to the supervisor.

Band C

An educational leader interested in professional growth and career, committed to a continuing relationship with Exempli Gratia Academy and the larger profession. A person who has demonstrated commitment to students and who is open to learning from a broadening circle of professional relationships inside and outside the school in a particular discipline area or in curriculum and teaching. To progress to Band D, the teacher must successfully complete the criteria in Band B and C and at least four of the following:

- present an advanced or experimental lesson to colleagues each year

- lead a group that provides professional collaboration (e.g., Critical Friends, Professional Learning Community)

- present a session at a national or regional educational conference

- chair a faculty committee

- develop and deliver a curriculum or program that serves to enhance the lives of Exempli Gratia Academy students and community members

- acquire professional certification in an area related to the teacher's discipline

- serve on an association visiting or accreditation team

Decision point: When the teacher believes that he or she is ready to progress to Band D (after at least three years in Band C) based on criteria, the teacher must submit a self-evaluation and band progression report to his or her supervisor.

Band D

An expert well-versed in the research and best practice methods of his or her discipline. An educator who draws students and other educators to him or her; highly respected by students and faculty alike, a teacher of teachers. A model of excellence and curiosity. A passionate keeper of the school vision, a paragon of the core values of Exempli Gratia Academy, a champion of the strategic plan, and a well-rounded, well-respected member of the community. This professional's presence is felt throughout all areas of the school, formally and informally. To retain membership in Band D, the educator is expected to:

- assist the Department Chair in guiding the growth of junior faculty members

- participate in several of the following each year:

  - teach a "master's course" lesson on an advanced or experimental educational topic to peers

  - present at a national or regional conference on a topic related to his or her discipline

  - publish a relevant article or research study in a journal

  - achieve advanced certification in a field related to his or her discipline

  - develop and deliver a curriculum or program that serves to enhance the lives of Exempli Gratia Academy students and community members

  - serve on or lead an association visiting or accreditation team.

Build choice into the bands (e.g., a faculty member must meet at least four of five or six requirements to move to the next band). This increases teachers' intrinsic motivation by enabling them to act on their passions and interests rather than being overly restricted by criteria that may not be meaningful to them.

Require faculty members wishing to move to a higher band to formally apply and present a professional growth portfolio demonstrating forward progression. Requiring concrete deliverables to progress from band to band helps teachers recognize the serious purpose (increases contribution and student impact) behind the band structure, rather than as a set of easily attained criteria that every teacher passes through without particular effort or commitment.

The Question of Naming Bands

Give careful consideration when naming the bands (such as Novice or Experienced). There are two schools of thought on this. Some schools prefer to use general labels such as Band A or Range A. This way, no faculty members assigned to any particular band feels dispirited or demotivated by their assignment (i.e., "How can I still be considered an 'Apprentice' after all these years?").

Conversely, other schools may find the bands' criteria serve as a guide and motivator to the teachers as they gain in skill level, impact, and contribution to the school's life and of their students and colleagues. This may be reason for the school to name the bands. One strong example is:

Band I (Learn)

Band II (Commit)

Band III (Lead)

Band IV (Give Back)

In this example, the band names clearly communicate the focus, purpose, and expectations of the teachers in each band.

Ultimately, the Head must determine which approach best fits the school's culture and values.

Assigning Faculty Members to Bands

Once the bands and criteria are established, the School Head and the academic administrators must assign each teacher to a band. Accomplish this by reviewing each teacher's current contributions and activities against the criteria of the bands. Many assignments will be straightforward (e.g., a first-year teacher straight out of graduate school to Band A and an eight-year veteran who regularly attends and presents at conferences, engages in action research, and chairs faculty committees to Band C). Other assignments may require more reflection (e.g., a 15-year veteran, a candidate for Band C based on past contributions and activities, whose contribution level has decreased in recent years should now be slotted in Band B). Base assignments solely on band criteria and contribution factors, with current salaries playing no role in band assignments.

Attaching Dollars to Each Band

After the design team establishes the bands and criteria to the Head's satisfaction, give the project to the Business Manager and Head (with budgetary support from the Board) to assign dollars (representing annual salaries) to each band. This may occur at the same time the academic administrators assign individual teachers to bands.

Continuing our Exempli Gratia Academy example, the financial component of the broadband structure might look like this chart.

Table 9.2

Exempli Gratia Academy Broadband Scale

Band A	$50,000 – $58,000
Band B	$56,000 – $69,000
Band C	$65,000 – $80,000
Band D	$74,000 – $92,000

Note: As with previous charts, the salary figures shown are provided for illustration purposes only. Schools should not consider these figures benchmarks, recommendations, or targets in any way.

When attaching dollars to the band levels, the minimum and maximum salaries at the extreme ends of the structure generally conforms to the current salaries present in the school. Salary ranges should overlap between bands, giving the administrator flexibility when placing each teacher in a band. That way, teachers have the opportunity for salary growth within their current band, as well as when moving from band to band.

The Importance of Strategic Planning and Strategic Financial Planning

A move to a broadbanding system requires attention to the school's strategic financial plan (or creation of one). After assigning faculty members to the bands, the Business Office can calculate the salary cost to achieve conformity to the band structure. For example, imagine the school has been holding to minimal to zero increases for faculty members for the past three years because of declining enrollment. That means new hires during that time did not advance far in salary, but now have progressed to Band B. These teachers might require as much as a 15% increase to conform (from $50,000 to $56,000) to the new bands. This percentage is likely higher than the school's expense gradient on the strategic financial plan.

Schools often reexamine their marketplace competitiveness at the same time, seeking to offer salary bands that make them more attractive to potential and current faculty members. It is not uncommon, especially after a period of limited increases that tracked at or below inflation, for schools to find they need to increase salaries 10% across the board. This is unlikely to be possible in a single budget year.

Whole-faculty salary adjustments, combined with the band assignment process, require careful financial planning. This analysis for total cost and associated strategic financial planning must be conducted before announcing the salary bands and their date of implementation. Otherwise, the school might discover that, although the growth and evaluation process and the faculty culture are "ready" for merit pay, the budget might not be.

Using the Bands: Movement from Band to Band

From an administrative perspective, when teachers are ready to progress to a new band, the Head has complete discretion regarding where a teacher is placed. Consider the following example.

- A teacher earning $75,000 in Band C is approved to move to B and D.
- Her salary already exceeds the low end of Band D, so no particular salary increase is necessary to get her into the band.
- Therefore, the administrator is free to determine the appropriate salary, from the current salary up to the band maximum of $92,000.
- In this case, the administrator might choose to set the teacher's new salary at $78,000 in the year she moves from Band C to Band D.
- This action has two significant results.
  1. The teacher's performance contribution is recognized as being at a Band D level.
  2. The teacher, previously at the upper end of Band C with limited salary growth potential, now has broad growth potential (i.e., $14,000 until she hits the current maximum of the band, with the maximum likely to progress upward over the years).

Using the Bands: Red-Circling

A key benefit of the band structure is that it gives the Head guidance (in the form of parameters and boundaries) on salary movement without being too rigid. Altering the above example slightly, say the teacher's current salary is $81,000 instead of $75,000, and she is clearly a Band C—not a Band D-level performer. In fact, her contribution has decreased over recent years. In this case, her $81,000 salary exceeds the maximum of Band C (which is $80,000).

Such situations are likely to occur during the first few years of using a band system (and even afterward, if teachers choose to ratchet down their performance level because of lifestyle commitments). In this case, the school would likely "red-circle" the teacher and discontinue salary increases, until:

- the teacher's contribution rebounds and warrants moving her up to Band D. (Here she would be within the bounds of the band's salary range and would not need to be red-circled or limited in salary growth for quite some time.); or

- the dollar ranges associated with each band are increased and the teacher again falls within the range of Band C (and once again has room for salary growth while remaining in that band).

By establishing criteria under which a faculty member can enter and move within the bands, the school places appropriate constraints on the administrator's discretion and provides balance between holding to a rigid system and using unfettered discretion.

Annual Salary Decisions Within a Broadbanding System

Once the broadbanding system is in place, the Head, and the academic and financial Leadership Team members, if appropriate, have decisions to make annually for each faculty member.

- For those faculty members staying within their current band this year, what is an appropriate increase?

- For those faculty members who have applied and been approved to move up in band this year, what is an appropriate pay level?

Depending on the analysis level in which the school chooses to engage, several factors influence the answers. This includes where the teacher's salary stands relative to the band in which he or she resides, the salaries of others in the same band, and relative impact compared to others in the band.

Comparing Salaries Within the Band

The first two factors (i.e., assessing where the teacher's salary stands relative to the band's boundaries and the salaries of others in the band) are easily determined by creating a chart listing all teachers in order of salary. The following example includes Exempli Gratia Academy faculty assigned to Band C.

Table 9.2

Exempli Gratia Academy Band C Salaries

Note: Band C ranges from $65,000 to $80,000.

Faculty Member	Salary	Comments
Nelson	$84,500	Because Nelson and Martinez exceed Band C's $80,000 maximum, they will likely be red-circled until such time as either the band maximum increases above their salary or they progress to Band D based on achievement of band criteria.
Martinez	$80,200	
Wisinski	$78,400	Because Wisinski, and D'Angelo are relatively close to the top of the band, their annual increase will likely be modest until they are ready to progress to Band D.
D'Angelo	$77,100	
Christiansen	$72,800	Since Christiansen, Anderson, Hale, and Sandstrom are in the middle of the band, the school can provide normal salary increases based on the relative contribution level. For example, if they demonstrate particularly strong impact, they might receive an increase of 6% this year— or, a relatively minimal contribution (while still within the band criteria) might generate only a 2% increase. This assumes the school's salary budget allows for an average of 4% in salary increases. As they approach the band's top in future years, though, they can expect their salary growth to slow (even with maximum contribution), until they are ready to move up to Band D.
Anderson	$72,500	
Hale	$72,100	
Sandstrom	$71,900	
LaBelle	$66,800	Being at the low end of the band, even more salary growth potential exists for LaBelle than it does for her four colleagues immediately above.
Gilbert	$62,800	Since Gilbert and Esposito are below the minimum of the band, they can expect increases this year that bring them at least to the band minimum
Esposito	$62,100	

Increasing the Salary Bands

Over time, it becomes necessary to increase the salary bands. As cost of living and the market drive up salaries for beginning teachers, the low end of Band A (the floor) must also increase for the school to offer competitive starting salaries.

The floor value of Band A is then affected by inflation and the school's desire to remain within a certain range of the competition for mission-aligned human resources. The school should plan for increases to the floor of its lowest salary band annually in line with cost-of-living increases in the area. This necessarily "compresses" the lowest band over time.

Similarly, the ceiling of the school's top level must also change over time. Imagine a teacher in Band D, a 30-year veteran who is still a top teacher and continues to earn high raises through his contribution and impact. At some point this teacher earns at the top level for that band. While his salary should never exceed the definition for Band D, it is unfair and unwise to hold him artificially to no raises simply because he has reached the band ceiling. While caps provide important cost controls, a lack of increases can quickly become a "dis-satisfier" for those who perform and do not see raises that others earn. Clearly, the band would need to be extended.

Schedule a review of the top salary band's ceiling value every four years, to coincide with the school's quadrennial strategic planning and strategic financial planning process. With a new floor to the school's lowest band (adjusted annually) and a new ceiling to the highest band, make adjustments to the other bands accordingly. During this process, the school must attend to the width and overlap of the salary levels as was done when the bands were first created. Note any outliers and "red-circle" faculty members to determine any special costs that might be incurred.

Compensation typically accounts for 65%–75% of a day school's annual expenses. Tying this process to strategic financial planning best prepares the school for any adjustments that occur because of the reformulated bands and are outside the school's historical expense gradient.

Before Taking the Plunge: Reassessing Readiness for Broadbanding

As the foregoing examples demonstrate, broadbanding structures require considerably more planning and preparation than other compensation approaches. Putting a broadbanding structure in place is a significant undertaking for any school, given the potential impact on the school's culture, finances, and operation. We urge schools to assess carefully their readiness before beginning this journey.

Four factors are necessary prerequisites for successful implementation of broadbanding.

1. The banding system must be regarded as fair and accurate. Teachers must understand what defines each band—and must regard the process for moving up the bands as fair and accurate. Without this, any connection of pay to faculty contribution will likely have a disastrous impact on the faculty culture.

2. The faculty culture must have a professional growth ethos. Teachers must be positively engaged in professional growth before implementing broadbanding. Again, not because the teacher's annual growth plan is connected to the banding system, but because the school's faculty culture may be one of entitlement rather than one committed to continual progress. If so, teachers will not eagerly embrace a system that helps them progress to higher levels of achievement. The culture must be changed before any broadbanding efforts can be successful.

3. The school's Board must operate strategically. Trustees must understand and plan for the impact that broadbanding can have on tuition. They must be willing to adjust tuition to provide funds for improving salaries. In addition, the Board must commit to establishing adequate funding for a proper management structure.

4. A well-defined Leadership Team must be in place to support teachers adequately. In most schools, the Head must be supported in coaching and mentoring of teachers by Division Heads, Department Chairs, or the like. If adequate management staff isn't in place, there is little chance the broadbanding system will be credible in the eyes of the faculty.

Broadbanding can be an effective strategy to address competitive faculty salaries, reward professional growth, and build institutional effectiveness. However, not every school should implement this strategy—and even fewer should attempt to do so without years of preparation. Assessing and understanding the particular school's current culture, management systems, and readiness are essential before beginning a broadbanding system.

Assessment of the School's Faculty Culture, Readiness for Implementation, and Implementation Outcomes

Faculty culture is one of the most important elements that the administration can drive in a school. The number one factor for parents and students when choosing which school to attend is the presence of a "safe, caring community." Teachers largely contribute to that sense of atmosphere parents and student seek. Faculty culture is also the top factor among teachers when choosing a place of employment. ISM research has found that it positively correlates to student performance, the perception of the executive leader, and enrollment demand.

This chapter offers suggestions on how the school can assess how effectively each process is operating, once implemented, and determine what cumulative effect these processes have on the school's faculty culture.

We have two purposes in mind.

■ Just as it is important for faculty members to grow continually and enhance their skills and performance, it is vital for the school (through its administration) to improve its employee programs, processes, and interactions. This way, the school can continue to attract, develop, retain, and inspire the highest-quality teachers possible to deliver its mission to its students. By assessing each program and process, schools can continually work to refine these processes, raising their excellence to the highest level attainable.

■ All the school's employee-related interactions serve to shape the school's faculty culture. A healthy culture—one in which teachers focus on creating predictable and supportive environments for students, as well as one in which they perceive the administration as being predictable and supportive toward them—is a primary correlate with student performance, satisfaction, and enthusiasm. Thus, assessing the culture helps the Leadership Team ensure the school is heading in the right direction, toward long-term success and sustained viability.

General Approaches to the Assessment and Monitoring of Processes and Culture

Faculty-related processes and the faculty culture may be assessed and monitored in two primary ways:

– anecdotally—such as through stories, vignettes, and anecdotes gained through the academic administrators' interactions, observations, and collaboration with individual teachers and groups of faculty in all aspects of their jobs inside and outside the classroom; and

– formally (and statistically)—through surveys of the faculty as a whole, as well as surveys of individual teachers or groups of teachers impacted by particular programs or processes.

Anecdotal Observations and Impressions

The Head can easily gather anecdotal observations of the success or impact of particular processes or programs by simply asking questions, inviting reflection, and soliciting responses at regular faculty meetings and Leadership Team meetings. Questions might include the following.

- What does the "temperature" of the faculty seem to be at the moment?

- What common concerns, irritations, high points, or success stories are you experiencing and talking about?

- How passionately are you (or your direct reports) engaged in your professional growth projects this year?

- How did you (or your direct reports) react to the performance evaluation discussions, professional growth and renewal meetings, etc., this year?

- What "side effects" have you observed resulting from implementation of our process?

- What evidence of impact do we have?

Questions for administrators only

How are we progressing with our hiring process this year? Do our top candidates seem stronger or weaker than in prior years? Do we seem more or less at risk for losing top candidates than we were in previous years? How are candidates reacting to our interview questions and processes?

How often have you observed and engaged with your teachers? Was it often enough to have a storehouse of anecdotes and observations to draw from?

The upside of anecdotal feedback is that it is relatively quick and easy to gain. In response to these questions, opinions and observations are likely to come gushing out from the teachers and academic administrators. The information shared is often rich with nuance and perspective that help unravel issues. This should be true if an environment of trust exists between teachers and administrators, where candid opinions and sensitive issues can be shared in confidence.

The downside is that the feedback may not be representative. In research parlance, it may lack validity and generalizability. Judgment is needed to discern whether it accurately represents faculty opinion as a whole or just the opinions of those who spoke up. Similarly, judgment is needed to know if what was reported was true; stated because it was "socially desirable"; or conversely, the product of an overly biased opinion. As with any other area, management must assess the relative weight and importance of each story with respect to the faculty environment and culture. Leadership must be aware of selection and confirmation biases that may also shade how management arrives at a conclusion.

Formal Surveys

Divide formal surveys into two categories.

1. **Targeted Surveys:** Direct these short surveys to individuals or groups impacted by particular programs or processes (e.g., survey newly hired teachers about the impact of the induction program).

2. **Whole-Faculty Surveys:** Use these faculty-wide surveys to capture the collective opinions of all teachers, to help assess the school's culture and climate.

Formal surveys can be provided in paper or electronic form. If more sophistication and/or anonymity is needed, quickly design them using an online survey software program. Similarly, they can be conducted in-house, or third-party survey vendors can be contracted, which may boost the faculty's confidence in the anonymity of the surveys.

Targeted Surveys (Processes and Programs)

A handful of targeted surveys are sketched out below (Example 10.1) that schools can use with various segments of the faculty population to gain feedback on components of the Comprehensive Faculty Development Model (CFD). Assessing the survey results helps the school know how predictable and supportive (or not) its programs and processes are, as considered from the faculty members' perspective.

All surveys can, of course, include space for comments and explanations, as well as yes/no and rating or ranking answers.

Note: Under each survey we have provided a mini-action plan, to help spur thinking on the ways in which the particular survey results may be used.

Example 10.1

> **New Hire "Nuts-and-Bolts" Survey**
>
> Shortly after a new faculty "class cohort" comes on board, the school could survey teachers to make sure they have the information and tools they need.
>
> 1. I have received keys or access codes to all rooms or equipment that I need in my role. (Yes, No)
>
> 2. I have communicated my payroll preferences (e.g., 10 month or 12 month pay cycle, if applicable) to the Business Office. (Yes, No)
>
> 3. I have provided payroll with my banking information for direct deposit purposes. (Yes, No)
>
> 4. I have completed my benefits enrollment forms and submitted all forms to the Business Office (Yes, No)

5. I have received a copy of the faculty and employee handbook. (Yes, No)

6. I have read the faculty and employee handbook and understand the policies and procedures that apply to me. (Yes, No)

Action Plan: Depending on the responses, the Head might confer with the Business Manager, HR Director, or other individuals responsible for processing incoming employees and determine an appropriate plan of action. This plan might include ensuring that all necessary documents, forms, resources, etc., are provided to the new employees promptly, if this is not currently the case.

Post-Induction Process Survey

Send this to new faculty members shortly after they complete the school's induction process.

1. The induction program helped me understand the school's mission. (Strongly agree, Somewhat agree, Neutral, Somewhat disagree, Strongly disagree)

2. The induction program helped me understand my classroom responsibilities. (Strongly agree, Somewhat agree, Neutral, Somewhat disagree, Strongly disagree)

3. The induction program helped me understand my cocurricular (e.g., coaching and advising) responsibilities. (Strongly agree, Somewhat agree, Neutral, Somewhat disagree, Strongly disagree)

4. I am aware of the expectations and criteria on which I will be evaluated. (Strongly agree, Somewhat agree, Neutral, Somewhat disagree, Strongly disagree)

5. I am confident that I know where to go or whom to approach when I need an answer about school policies and procedures or my job responsibilities. (Strongly agree, Somewhat agree, Neutral, Somewhat disagree, Strongly disagree)

6. I have met with my coach or mentor regularly enough to foster mutual trust. (Strongly agree, Somewhat agree, Neutral, Somewhat disagree, Strongly disagree)

7. I have identified and written my professional goals for me to work on this year and communicated the goals and resources needed to my coach or mentor. (Strongly agree, Somewhat agree, Neutral, Somewhat disagree, Strongly disagree)

8. I feel that I need more information about the following topics, issues, and procedures to do my job better at this time. (Please describe.)

Action Plan: The Head and administrators responsible for the induction program would meet to determine ways to strengthen the school's program for the following year. This might include establishing an administrator-faculty committee to study and enhance the induction process. The school could also follow up with recent hires to proactively answer any questions or concerns that might not have been addressed fully during the induction process. (See Chapter Four: Mission-Based Onboarding: Orientation and Induction for details.)

Post-Periodic Review Survey

Send this to all teachers immediately after a periodic review is completed.

1. My supervisor met with me to discuss my periodic performance review. (Yes, No)

2. I was provided with a copy of my evaluation. (Yes, No)

3. I feel that my evaluation fairly and objectively reflected my performance of the Essential Expectations (Strongly agree, Somewhat agree, Neutral, Somewhat disagree, Strongly disagree)

4. I had the opportunity to ask questions and voice my opinions during the evaluation meeting. (Strongly agree, Somewhat agree, Neutral, Somewhat disagree, Strongly disagree)

Action Plan: This survey can serve as an effective follow-up mechanism for the Leadership Team. Anything less than 100% "Yes" answers to the first two statements would be cause to follow up with the direct supervisors to ensure the evaluation process is carried out appropriately with all faculty members (absent any mitigating circumstances). Any degree of negative response to statements 3 and 4 may warrant retraining for supervisors regarding the evaluation process, and may call for more general communication to teachers about the aims and processes of the evaluation program.

Professional Growth and Renewal Program Survey

Send this to all returning teachers between the fourth and sixth week of the school year.

1. I am aware of my required responsibility for pursuing professional growth and renewal this year and throughout my career at the school. (Strongly agree, Somewhat agree, Neutral/uncertain, Somewhat disagree, Strongly disagree)

2. I am aware of the professional growth and renewal opportunities available to me at the school. (Strongly agree, Somewhat agree, Neutral, Somewhat disagree, Strongly disagree)

3. I have completed my personal reflection. (Yes, No)

4. I have written my professional growth and renewal plan and communicated it, along with necessary resources, to my coach or mentor. (Yes, No)

5. My coach or mentor has approved my growth and renewal plan. (Yes, No)

6. I have shared my goals with others in my department or professional learning community. (Yes, No)

Action Plan: This survey is designed to assist the Leadership Team in understanding how completely the policies and processes for professional growth have taken hold within the faculty. Negative responses to the first two questions would be cause for follow-up with the direct supervisors to assure communication has occurred. The final four items help assess where all faculty members are in the process.

Professional Growth and Renewal Program Year-End Survey

Send this to all teachers at the end of the school year.

1. I made satisfactory progress on (at least) two professional growth and renewal plan goals at some point this school year. (Yes, No)

2. My participation in professional growth and renewal directly benefited my students this year. (Strongly agree, Somewhat agree, Neutral, Somewhat disagree, Strongly disagree)

3. I believe my participation in the growth and renewal cycle benefitted my colleagues this year. (Strongly agree, Somewhat agree, Neutral, Somewhat disagree, Strongly disagree)

4. My coach or mentor and I regularly engaged in the "ongoing conversation" helping to advance my teaching. (Strongly agree, Somewhat agree, Neutral, Somewhat disagree, Strongly disagree)

5. I have ample information on which to reflect to create my next set of goals (OR I have already engaged in a new set of growth goals that will carry over next year). (Strongly agree, Somewhat agree, Neutral, Somewhat disagree, Strongly disagree)

Action Plan: This survey helps schools understand the frequency with which growth goals are being achieved and their perceived impact on students and colleagues. Lack of agreement on any of the final four items in the context of agreement on the first item suggests a culture of compliance has been created, rather than transformation. Striving for more inspiring goals or examination of resources (time and money) may be necessary.

Compensation Program Survey

Send this to all teachers after contracts and band placement are communicated in the spring (where broadbanding is used).

1. My supervisor communicated my new salary for next year to me. (Yes, No)

2. My supervisor clearly explained how my new salary was derived. (Strongly agree, Somewhat agree, Neutral, Somewhat disagree, Strongly disagree)

3. I believe that my salary is appropriate with respect to my contribution to the school. (Strongly agree, Somewhat agree, Neutral, Somewhat disagree, Strongly disagree)

4. I believe that my salary is comparable to what I would receive for a similar role at a competing private school. (Strongly agree, Somewhat agree, Neutral, Somewhat disagree, Strongly disagree)

5. I am aware of the opportunities available to me to increase my pay in the future. (Strongly agree, Somewhat agree, Neutral, Somewhat disagree, Strongly disagree)

Action Plan: Responses to statements 1, 2, and 5 will indicate how clearly the school is communicating about its compensation program. Statements 3 and 4 may provide the Head with an early indication of whether salaries may play a role in teacher-retention issues.

ISM's Research-Based Whole-Faculty Surveys

As noted in the "anecdotal survey" section above, an engaged observer doesn't require a formal instrument to gain a general sense of how a faculty culture is progressing. He or she can often get a partial feel just by being around and in it for a short period of time. That said, most schools find it helpful to assess the culture in a more structured and systematic way, as well. For this purpose, ISM developed two faculty survey instruments:

- the **Faculty Culture Profile** (FCP), based on our research on the factors that correlate most strongly with student performance, satisfaction, and enthusiasm; and

- the **Faculty Experience Survey** (FES), which assesses the experienced predictability and support through the evaluation process.

ISM's Research for School Management (RSM) and Student Experience Study (SES) research studies identified and reaffirmed the strong correlation between student performance, satisfaction, and enthusiasm and a healthy faculty culture. This is defined as a culture in which teachers:

- are focused on continual professional growth and are constantly engaged in discussing the difference-makers in the lives of students;

- are striving every day to provide a predictable and supportive environment for students; and

- perceive the administration actively cares about and supports their needs.

These factors operate on individual as well as collective levels. Just as each teacher must pursue his or her own growth and renewal plan, he or she must be able to trust that each fellow teacher is just as focused and dedicated to that professional growth goal. One happy result is that in such cultures, the weight of the culture shifts strongly to the positive. Negative or bitter teachers will be held accountable, and if not terminated, spin out to the margins—finding their behavior perceived as inappropriate within the core, positive culture—and increasingly have less and less impact on the whole without correction of such an attitude.

Over the long term, a teacher can't rise above the culture of the whole. If most teachers aren't actively engaged in professional growth, the ones who embrace that goal eventually become pulled down and dispirited by the overall faculty culture. This leads to bitterness, learned helplessness, and other damaging factors and effects.

The ingredients of a healthy faculty culture become evident when the community begins to notice broad-based examples of:

- – commitment by individuals to their own growth and career;
- – whole-faculty commitment to common goals and purposes (evidenced by a common understanding and practice of professional excellence);
- – teachers' desire to grow in support of one another (evidenced by collegiality and collaboration); and
- – administrators providing high levels of predictability and support, as experienced by the faculty as a whole.

The instruments described below allow the Leadership Team to better assess the strength and health of its faculty culture through use of a formal survey.

The Faculty Experience Survey

The Faculty Experience Survey (Example 10.2) measures teachers' attitudes and opinions on the level of predictability and support they experience from their administrators through the evaluation process. This gets at the focus of this book—creating a healthy environment in which faculty members understand how they are evaluated and trust that process.

The FES is a 10-item questionnaire comprised of two dimensions: "predictability" and "supportiveness." The scores on each dimension are the mean averages of the faculty's responses to the five items within each dimension. Plot those averages on a matrix (see Figure 10.1), with supportiveness along the horizontal axis and predictability along the vertical access. The point plotted by the two scores determines the school's current "quadrant."

There are four main areas on the matrix: Optimal Performance Quad, Predictability Quad, Supportiveness Quad, and Toxic Quad. "Optimal" is defined as above the upper cutoff for predictability and supportiveness dimensions and indicates the school's evaluation processes are perceived to be consistent, fair, and helpful. "Toxic" is defined as below the lower cutoff (which we call the "toxic line") for both dimensions and suggests serious concerns for the school's leadership in driving a healthy faculty culture. The Predictability and Supportiveness quadrants reflect the presence of averages above the upper cutoff score on one dimension and below the upper cutoff score on the other.

There are three other areas of note. The Undifferentiated section means that scores are below the upper cutoff scores, but no so far below as to warrant being in the Toxic Quad. Since neither dimension is prominent, as such, the quality of the faculty experience is unclear. There are also two Borderline areas, defined as being above the toxic line on one dimension (but not above the upper cutoff), and below the toxic line on the other. These areas describe a culture "on the border" of being in the Predictable or Supportiveness quads, but not worthy of inclusion there.

Figure 10.1

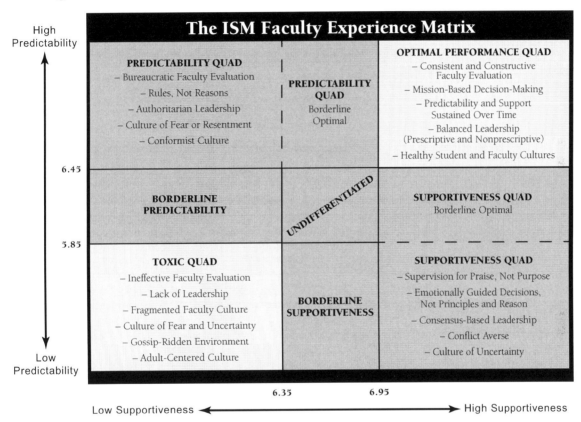

Note: The normal cutoff scores noted on this figure are those used at the point of publication.

Example 10.2

The Faculty Experience Survey

Consider in your responses only the three most recent months unless otherwise instructed. Score each statement on a 1 to 9 scale with "1" being "not true at all" and "9" being "exactly true." The focus in this survey is on the overall climate of the school; the focus is not on the individual. Each question begins with the phrase, "I and my colleagues." Although you cannot speak with complete accuracy for your colleagues, for the purpose of this survey, please provide your perspective as well as your impressions of your colleagues' perspectives on the issues.

| 1 | 2 | 3 | 4 | 5 | 6 | 7 | 8 | 9 |

Not true of us at all   *Exactly true of us*

I and my colleagues

1. understand exactly how we are evaluated.

2. view our evaluation procedures as consistent (i.e., predictable).

3. view our evaluation procedures as constructive (i.e., helpful).

4. view our faculty culture as appropriately supportive (as evidenced by collegial interaction).

5. view our school's administrative culture (i.e., the collective attitude of all our administrative staff members, including those in the Business Office, Development Office, Admission Office, and so on) as appropriately supportive of the faculty: i.e., wishing our success and striving to support us in our efforts.

6. find the administrator(s) who supervises and/or evaluates us is highly supportive of us: i.e., hopes for our success and is focused on our growth and renewal as professionals.

7. agree the administrator(s) who supervises and/or evaluates us provides us with accurate reinforcement regarding our performance as faculty members.

8. agree the administrator(s) who supervises and/or evaluates us demonstrates consistent responses on a daily basis, i.e., we find that we know what to expect from her or him in all situations.

9. agree the administrator(s) who supervises us and/or evaluates us provides clarity of expectations.

10. agree the administrator(s) who supervises us and/or evaluates us is eager to assist us in meeting those expectations.

Scoring

A. Average the mean scores for items 3, 4, 5, 6, and 10 to obtain the supportiveness score.

B. Average the mean scores for items 1, 2, 7, 8, and 9 to obtain the predictability score.

C. Go to the ISM Faculty Experience Matrix (Figure 10.1) and use the cutoff scores along the corresponding axis to plot the school's current quadrant.

The Faculty Culture Profile

The Faculty Culture Profile (Example 10.3) is a 20-item questionnaire designed to assess the school's culture, rather than teacher satisfaction. ISM's research has demonstrated that high scores on the FCP predict high student performance, satisfaction, and enthusiasm. The survey contains a broad range of items about how each respondent perceives that "I and my colleagues" treat and relate to students, one another, and administrators. It also includes perception of their professional development efforts and therefore is helpful in monitoring the effectiveness of CFD implementation.

Example 10.3

The ISM Faculty Culture Profile

All faculty members are asked to answer the following, using the following scale for each question.

| 1 | 2 | 3 | 4 | 5 | 6 | 7 | 8 | 9 |

Not true of us at all   *Exactly true of us*

I and my colleagues:

- find ways to make it obvious to all students that we wish them success every day, in school and outside of school;
- find ways to make it obvious to all students that we want them to become better, more ethical people (in ways consistent with our school's stated purposes and projected outcomes for our graduates);
- set clearly articulated standards for student academic performance;

– set reasonable, defensible standards for student behavior;

– are continually alert to displays of unkindness among students;

– conduct ourselves in confrontations with students in ways that leave students' dignity intact regardless of the nature of the issue or infraction;

– individually and collectively demonstrate believably high levels of enthusiasm for teaching/learning and for the content of our studies;

– demonstrate through words and actions a genuine, believable commitment to the school, its purposes, its leadership, and one another;

– are glad to arrive at school and to see our students each day;

– create predictable assessments (not to be confused either with "simple" or "easy" assessments); our students can rely on the preparation we offer them;

– provide fair, reliable, understandable grade and reward structures for our students; our students are led to understand why they receive the grades they receive—high or low—and thereby to see how improvement, if they will seek it, might be possible;

– enforce our rules justly, fairly, consistently;

– are able to present ourselves each day in ways that will be seen by our students as consistent and reliable (i.e., unaffected by outside-of-school problems);

– individually and collectively pursue career-long professional development as a foremost priority;

– have mastered at least one pedagogical approach—not necessarily the same one for all of us—that is supported by reliable, contemporary research outcomes;

– are in casual conversations with one another, and those conversations tend to be constructive, upbeat, and professional;

– have great respect for our division and/or school administrators;

– find that our division and/or school administrators are highly supportive of our division's and/or school's faculty;

– find that our division or school administrators are highly supportive of our division's and/or school's students; and

– find that our division and/or school administrators are highly supportive of our division's or school's parents.

Scoring

There are two ways to score the FCP.

1. Averages Method: A more traditional method, which requires knowledge of statistics to make inferences year-to-year.

   ■ Create averages for each item.

   ■ Compare the averages year-to-year, using your initial averages as a self-referenced benchmark to note trends. (Remember, you may not compare averages collected at different times of year).

   ■ Use statistical analysis to judge whether a change in average from one year to the next is statistically significant.

2. "At the Good End": An easier method, which yields a single value that relates to the viewpoint of the preponderance of the faculty and reduces the impact of intensely negative outliers on the total outcome.

   ■ For each item, calculate the percentage of responses that earned a 7, 8, or 9 ("at the good end").

   ■ Track the total number of items out of 20 that reach the 75% criterion and compare that number year-to-year, division-to-division.

   ■ Track percentages for each item year-to-year if desired.

Note that ISM uses both methods in tandem when assessing faculty culture to provide richer data for interpretive purposes.

Frequency and Timing of the Faculty Culture Profile

Since ISM first developed its Faculty Culture Profile in the 1990s, we have recommended that schools administer the instrument as follows.

■ Survey faculty members using the Faculty Culture Profile three times each academic year (approximately November, February, and May).

■ The three-times-per-year model has been suggested roughly to correspond with the emotional cycle in a school year—from its most positive (November), to its low point (midwinter), to its recovery (spring).

■ Following this approach, distribute the survey at the same times each year (e.g., the first week of November). This way you can compare the results from year to year (i.e., November compared to the previous November, February compared to the previous February).

This method has been used successfully by schools that follow it scrupulously as part of their faculty-administrator calendar. Other schools, though, may find that this frequency generates "survey fatigue" among faculty members and administrators, decreasing enthusiasm for the process and the reliability of the results. For these schools, once or twice per year is an option.

The School Culture Team

The administration can distribute, collect, score, and report the results of the Faculty Culture Profile each time—an efficient and easy approach. However, task a group of teachers with giving and scoring the FCP. Specifically, form a School Culture Team (SCT)—a group of credible and exemplary teacher-leaders. Task the SCT with distributing, collecting, scoring, and reporting the results back to the faculty. The advantage is that faculty members feel, right from the beginning, the connection of the survey to the faculty culture, i.e., "we are administering it to ourselves" (the teachers).

The SCT should also consider whether there are any issues that arise out of the FCP results, comparing year-to-year, and offer suggestions for improvement. The SCT would present the results and the feedback to the administration before sharing the results with the faculty. After reviewing the results with the faculty and soliciting feedback, the administration may begin to consider new initiatives to addresses issues or concerns.

The School Culture Team consists of three to seven members, depending on the school's size and number of divisions. It has the responsibility of monitoring and helping leadership guide faculty culture. The group must be:

- **strategically selected.** Members are leaders among the faculty, have a reputation for being positive, and are student-centered. At least one member must be highly capable of analyzing and presenting quantitative data;

- **data-informed.** The members work not from rumor, but on research-based measures of the school culture (e.g., results of the FCP) or formalized feedback channels;

- **solution-oriented.** This is not a "grievance committee" charged simply with voicing complaints to administrators. When issues arise, the group must also generate multiple solutions;

- **open to telling the truths of the culture.** The SCT must understand the varied perspectives existing within the entire culture—and must be able to see the view from teacher, student, and leadership perspectives. Open and honest feedback is essential to maintaining a healthy school culture. The SCT must be willing to voice feedback to the administration and fellow faculty members, even if it feels uncomfortable in the short term; and

– **highly collaborative.** This group must work with leadership and the faculty to generate solutions when appropriate.

The Student Experience Profile (SEP)

As the two instruments above measure the perception of predictability and support levels given and received by teachers, ISM also developed the SEP, an instrument designed to measure the level of predictability and support students feel they receive from teachers (Example 10.4). Conducting this survey in tandem with the FCP is an excellent way to compare how predictable and supportive the environment is from the faculty and the student points of view. (While the scale descriptors vary somewhat according to the question, 7, 8, and 9 are the "good end" of the scale as was seen in the FCP.)

Example 10.4

The Student Experience Profile (SEP)

| 1 | 2 | 3 | 4 | 5 | 6 | 7 | 8 | 9 |

Not accurate at all   *Fully accurate*

1. I have very much looked forward to coming to school every day of this grading period.

2. I have not seen or heard of unkind behavior—of anybody being "picked on" in any way at all—anywhere in our school during this grading period.

3. I find that I am proud of my school, and proud to be part of such a school.

4. It has been obvious to me that my teachers really want me to do well—in school and out of school.

5. My teachers have worked every day at helping me become a better, more ethical person, regardless of the subject they are teaching (math, science, English, history, etc.).

6. I have been very excited about what I've been studying this grading period (the course material itself, not the teaching of the material).

7. I'm so satisfied with my school, I'd certainly want to come here if my family and I could choose again.

---

8. Our assessments (tests, etc.) this grading period have included exactly what my teachers said they would include.

9. All the grades I received during this grading period—big tests, quizzes, papers, etc.—were exactly the grades I think I actually earned—no higher or lower.

10. I have been completely satisfied with the school's rules.

11. Our teachers have enforced the school's rules justly, fairly, and consistently.

12. I have known exactly what to expect from my teachers, every day. I have known just how they will react to anything we say or do.

Scoring

There are two ways to score the SEP.

1. Averages Method: A more traditional method, which requires knowledge of statistics to make inferences year-to-year.

   ■ Create averages for each item.

   ■ Compare the averages year-to-year, using your initial averages as a self-referenced benchmark to note trends. (Remember, you may not compare averages collected at different times of year).

   ■ Use statistical analysis to judge whether a change in average from one year to the next is statistically significant.

2. "At the Good End": An easier method, which yields a single value that relates to the viewpoint of the preponderance of the faculty and reduces the impact of intensely negative outliers on the total outcome.

   ■ For each item, calculate the percentage of responses that earned a 7, 8, or 9 ("at the good end").

   ■ Track the total number of items out of 12 that reach the 75% criterion and compare that number year-to-year, division-to-division.

   ■ Track percentages for each item year-to-year if desired.

Note that ISM uses both methods in tandem when assessing faculty culture to provide richer data for interpretive purposes.

The Survey Results: Now What?

As with all the surveys suggested in this chapter, the question Heads must ask in assessing the FES, FCP, and SEP results is, "Now what?" What can or should the Head do to address the faculty's feedback? This depends primarily on two factors:

- the particular outcomes and how they compare to the school's historical results; and

- any new or unusual events that occurred shortly before administering the survey and may have influenced the outcome (example: the midyear termination of a well-known faculty member).

As with many items on the Head's agenda, "what to do now" is a matter of judgment, discernment, and experience. Consider these factors.

- If faculty members rate themselves and their colleagues low on how students are treated (items No. 1 to 6), or if the SEP scores are low, an adult-centered culture may be prominent. Take immediate steps to reorient teachers to a student-centered or learner-centered approach. Changing this culture is also is likely to include dismissing toxic elements among your faculty members.

- If an underlying theme to teacher responses is, "I'm doing these things, but my colleagues aren't," this might suggest that:

  - they are right—other faculty members are not mission-inappropriate (which could require improved hiring practices and/or more vigorous corrective action); and/or

  - there are inadequate opportunities for faculty members to get to know and work with one another (i.e., rating others low because of lack of exposure to them). Address this by actively seeking and implementing teacher collaboration options (e.g., team teaching, knowledge socialization sessions).

- If teachers report low scores on rules and standards (items No. 10 to 12), it's essential to implement conversations about being fair and predictable while holding high standards. There may be reason to revisit content on how rules and fairness apply to discipline and grading in the school's handbooks.

- If teachers grade their colleagues highly but give low marks to the questions centering on trust of administrators or support from administrators (items No. 17 to 20), this might suggest a divide between the faculty and the administration in the school. This may come from a lack of interaction, engagement, and collaboration between the two groups. For example, administrators may have a reputation of never coming out of their offices, or administrators may only visit with teachers when there are problems to discuss. This may be addressed by proactively engaging faculty members in the types of coaching and mentoring relationships noted earlier.

- Low trust scores could indicate that Division Heads and Department Chairs are attempting to coach and mentor but need additional training. Or the ratings could indicate the school has some supervisors who are not well-suited to the demands of leadership of adults (as opposed to teaching children). The school may need to review the academic Leadership Team and consider whether all the members are well-positioned to succeed in their current roles, and then make any necessary changes.

There is, of course, an array of possible interpretations of survey results, just as there are any number of potential ways to address issues that are raised. Using the school's mission, culture, and values as the prism through which the results are viewed may assist the Head in determining his or her approach. The more frequently, passionately, and vibrantly the school's mission, culture, and values are articulated, the more predictable and supportive the environment becomes for teachers and students. Therein lies a key source of the school's ongoing success.

Drawing All the Threads Together

Returning to Covey's "begin with the end in mind" maxim, the end goal for all academic administrators is to have a thriving school where students:

- perform to the best of their ability;
- are highly engaged and satisfied with the school; and
- demonstrate great enthusiasm for the various aspects of the school.

If this is the result, then the vehicle—or means— is an engaged, collaborative faculty constantly seeking excellence.

This vehicle—the faculty—is best maintained by a Leadership Team that acts with great clarity, support, and respect for its teachers. To ensure the Leadership Team has successfully provided clarity, support, and respect, data must be obtained. While anecdotal data can be useful, survey-based data allows all voices to be heard, not just the loudest, most opinionated, and most frequently heard. Perhaps more important, data provides either direct feedback to implementation events (e.g., immediately after induction, after periodic review) or longitudinal data that show trajectory over time.

Steps to Implementing a New Teacher Evaluation Process

Successful implementation of any initiative requires careful planning and transparency. We have offered a comprehensive view of onboarding, growth and renewal, and evaluation. However, where do you start?

In a school where evaluation is new or where evaluation has been negative or inconsistent in the past, acknowledge the situation and include teachers in the conversation. Consider the following implementation steps.

Step 1: Assess the school's Purpose and Outcome Statements (P&O Statements). Create or update as necessary the three transformative elements: mission, Portrait of the Graduate (POG), and Characteristics of Professional Excellence (CPE). See Chapter Two: Purpose and Outcome Statements on development options and procedures. Expect this to take at least four to eight weeks to accomplish. The Board approves any changes to the mission, and this may extend the timing of the P&O development.

Step 2: Appoint a School Culture Team (SCT) to measure, monitor, and assist in solving faculty culture issues. The SCT has responsibility for administering, collecting, tabulating, and presenting the results of the school's faculty culture measures. It may also assist the administration in analyzing qualitative, quantitative, anecdotal, and formal data. The SCT serves as a liaison to the leadership to help monitor, maintain, and improve faculty culture.

Step 3: Assess the school's faculty culture to benchmark its current level of predictability and support. Establish a baseline by using ISM's Faculty Culture Profile (FCP) and Faculty Experience Survey (FES) to understand the whole culture and the faculty's current perception of the evaluation processes. (See Chapter Nine: Assessing the School's Faculty Culture and CFD Implementation.) Have the School Culture Team, appointed in Step 2, administer the FCP. The administration should distribute the FES anonymously and tabulate results.

Assess the school's culture from students' viewpoints. ISM's Student Experience Profile (SEP) is one measure that can be used to reflect students' experiences of the faculty culture. Students' viewpoints serve to validate or highlight important differences in perception.

At Step 3, make a decision. If the faculty culture is "good," then the school can proceed. If, however, the faculty culture is abysmal, give the SCT and division leadership time to deal with specific issues—unless, of course, what is at issue is a direct consequence of evaluation procedures that have led to:

  – powerful toxic teachers undermining the culture; or

  – the leadership's failure to craft a workable process.

In these cases, the toxic culture needs the immediate implementation of a new, mission-based, growth-focused, predictable and supportive, and student-centered faculty development process.

Step 4: Determine the school's Essential Expectations (EE). Create a team comprised of academic administrators and exemplary teachers to develop the school's Essential Expectations (or refine those that may exist). This list must include an item that addresses requiring teachers to engage in a professional development plan (i.e., No. 10 from ISM's list: "Authentically engage in self-reflection and annual development of a growth and renewal plan based on the Characteristics of Professional Excellence. This includes written goals and progress toward those goals"). Present the EE list to the School Head for final approval.

Step 5: In the school's strategic financial plan, allot 2% of operational expenses to faculty professional development (and an additional 1% for the administration and staff). If these percentages are not achievable, create a plan for providing sufficient funds to cover each teacher's development plan.

Step 6: Create a mentor-coach plan, being sure not to exceed 15 teachers per mentor (except for positions with primary responsibility, such as a Director of Professional Development). Emphasize among division leaders that developing the capacity of teachers is their primary responsibility, and make it part of how the School Head evaluates their performance. Establish that 25%–50% of their weekly time should be in broad service to faculty development. If more staff members are needed to allow for this, ensure additional positions are part of the school's strategic financial plan.

Step 7: Train coaches and mentors in how to be coaches and mentors. Being a coach or mentor is unlike being a supervisor. As such, people who serve in this role must learn and practice how to succeed. Plan for annual training, even for the most experienced. Remember that in CFD, teachers serve as pseudo-coaches of one another (e.g., as a Critical Friend or member of a Professional Learning Community). Being a good coach does not stop at facilitating the teacher's professional goals, but further entails being a model for teachers as they seek to coach one another.

Step 8: Update the school's faculty and employee handbook. Update the handbook(s) to include:

- new Purpose and Outcome statements;
- the policies and procedures for the new growth and evaluation procedures;
- Essential Expectations;
- copies of forms required; and
- reasons for termination that would not follow the "four-step corrective-action model" (or other, if modified by the school) outlined in this book.

The school's employment lawyer should look over any modifications.

Step 9: Find time each week for teachers to meet to drive their professional development goals. In Step 5, the school is expected to provide financial resources to support teacher growth and renewal. Here the school provides the perhaps more valuable resource of time. This may require a schedule modification or change, e.g., a late start once per week. Do not, however, set aside time after school for professional development. Most teachers are not at their creative best at day's end, and they are pulled in too many directions (coaching, tutoring, clubs) for this to be an effective time for professional development.

Step 10: Schedule an inspiring, brief kick-off meeting partially led by faculty members in which presenters share their development goals. Share the evaluation framework with the faculty and answer any questions about its intent and how it is to be used. This should be inspiring and hope-filled. Do not bog down in this session into the procedural aspects—although some people will want to take it in that direction. Emphasize the student-centeredness aspects and benefits to the teachers.

CFD should coexist with coaching and evaluation procedures for administrators as well. The growth and evaluation processes are substantially different at the administrative level. They have in common the provision of creating "two professional development goals," which may be appropriate to share with teachers to create a sense of shared purpose and experience.

Step 11: Hold a second meeting (or more) to share with the entire faculty new Purpose and Outcome Statements and Essential Expectations. The faculty should hear from leadership the meaning and importance of any P&O Statements (mission, Characteristics of Professional Excellence, and Portrait of the Graduate) and the Essential Expectations used for evaluation purposes. This might be a good time to provide the faculty with an updated faculty and employee handbook. Document receipt of the handbook.

Step 12: Set a meeting for each teacher with the person who will conduct his or her periodic evaluation. This meeting is to communicate Essential Expectations and any specific duties and responsibilities to be evaluated on a "meeting expectations" or "not meeting expectations" basis. Provide a time when the teacher might expect the first periodic review.

Step 13: Schedule one-to-one coach and mentor meetings for orientation to the growth and renewal process. Deliver procedural information in one-to-one meetings and conversations. The agenda items for this meeting include:

- informing teachers about how the growth and renewal process works and the role the coach plays;
- communicating the expectations of each faculty member;
- distributing forms (electronic or hard copy) for completing the written goals; and
- answering any questions.

Step 14: Officially log each teacher's goals and potential resources required. The form used to record the teacher's goals should be submitted to the coach or mentor. Mentors should provide this information to the Division Head for planning and knowledge purposes.

Step 15: Schedule mentor and coach gatherings to troubleshoot issues. All coaches and mentors should communicate regularly, as a group, to troubleshoot and cross-pollinate ideas. It is likely there will be more meetings and communication early in the process.

Step 16: Regularly log progress on each teacher's goals, with the understanding that they may be completed and new goals developed at any time of year.

Step 17: Schedule and complete periodic reviews. Evaluation supervisors should map out their planned periodic reviews to be sure they occur before contract renewal (early spring for those on an annual or less frequent review schedule). Similarly, they should schedule reviews for those on corrective action coming into the school year (held over from the previous year) and for new teachers (if the school decides to conduct more frequent reviews for new teachers).

Step 18: Review the impact. Leadership, including all coaches and mentors, should generate feedback to guide the program's improvement. Among the questions feedback should answer are:

- What went well?
- How might we improve?
- What is next?

Step 19: Repeat for two more years. Remain consistent with the process. Be sure to reassess faculty culture each year as directed. Minor tweaks to the procedures or the way certain aspects are carried out are welcomed, but consistency is one of the most important factors to establishing trust.

Step 20: After two years of implementation with strong faculty culture scores, consider the move to broadbanding. Assess the school's readiness and desire for implementation of a such a system. See Chapter Nine: Compensation for a description and implementation hints.

Note the preceding steps provide a general outline for the implementation of CFD. Schools will likely need to modify these steps as their particular situations warrant. However, it should provide a good "check" to be sure all bases are covered.

Legal Background and Compliance Issues

All school administrators must have a basic understanding of the key federal and state statutes that impact hiring, evaluation, pay, and termination practices in schools. They must carry out these processes in a legally compliant and effective manner.

The scope of this book's legal discussion extends solely to the laws of the United States. Private schools operating in other countries should seek counsel regarding their home country's employment and discrimination laws (which may differ from the regulations noted here). In the United States, laws are passed at the federal, state, and local levels.

Note that ISM is not a law firm and the contributing authors of this book are not attorneys. None of the following may be construed as legal advice. Rather, we present this information as a brief primer on basic employment law. All schools must establish an ongoing relationship with an employment attorney qualified in their state and to seek direct legal advice from this individual (or firm) on all employment matters.

Federal, State, and Local Laws Impacting Hiring, Evaluation, Reward, and Termination Practices

This discussion primarily concerns federal laws that impact employment practices—and, thus, that apply to all 50 states and the District of Columbia. School administrators should be aware, however, that the state in which the school operates may have passed other laws that provide additional rights, benefits, and protections to employees. These surpass federal law (i.e., state regulations cannot take away rights employees have under federal law but they may extend or expand those rights). The same is true for the localities (e.g., counties, cities, or other local jurisdictions).

For example, the Fair Labor Standards Act (FLSA) provides federal standards on minimum wage and overtime pay calculations. Certain states have gone beyond FLSA to set higher minimum wage (e.g., "living wage") and overtime provisions, as have certain cities. Consult with qualified legal counsel (i.e., an employment or labor attorney) about the laws and terms in their jurisdiction.

Title VII of the Civil Rights Act of 1964

The section of the groundbreaking civil rights era legislation known as Title VII is the foundation for several employment discrimination laws (detailed below). Title VII prohibits discrimination in employment with respect to an individual's race, color, sex, religion, national origin, or genetic information. Consider these categories "protected classes"—so named as they are explicitly protected against discrimination under the law.

Title VII is also the statute on which sexual harassment prohibitions are based. Many states and localities have designed additional protected classes such as medical condition, HIV status, sexual orientation, and gender identity. The number and definition of added classes protected by law vary considerably from state to state and from year to year. So, it is essential to know the protected classes for your state in a given year.

Every school should have an Equal Employment Opportunity (EEO) statement on its employment application, on the job posting page of its website, and in its employee handbook that states:

> *"The school is an equal opportunity employer that makes all decisions regarding employment, compensation, benefits, and all other terms and conditions of employment without regard to a candidate or employee's race, color, religion, sex, national origin, age, disability, veteran status, genetic information, or other characteristic protected by federal, state, or local law."*

Schools in states (or localities) providing additional protected-class statuses should include these in their EEO statement.

Faith-based schools should note that Title VII provides a specific exception regarding religion for faith-based organizations. If a faith-based school determines that—consistent with its mission—it will use religion as a hiring criterion for some (or all) positions in the school, it is legally permitted to do so. Eliminate the word "religion" from the EEO statement and add the following: "As a faith-based institution, the school reserves the right to use religion as a hiring criterion for selected positions, as permitted by law and consistent with the mission of the institution."

The Age Discrimination in Employment Act (ADEA) of 1967

The ADEA prohibits discrimination against employees or candidates aged 40 and older, and prohibits forced (age-based) retirement in most circumstances. A school may validly specify experience requirements where appropriate to the position (e.g., either two or four years of experience teaching AP classes for an AP chemistry position). It should never, however, set (verbally or in writing) age requirements or set experience requirements that can't be supported.

The school should make certain that it does not ask for a high school graduation year on its employment application—courts view this as a proxy for determining the candidate's age. Be careful not to use words such as "young," "mature," or similar age-implied phrases in employment advertisements.

The Equal Pay Act of 1963

Employers are prohibited from discriminating in pay decisions based on gender. One example of a violation of this law would be for a school to provide higher starting salaries to male teachers, because of their perceived status as heads of households, or to pay men more solely in an attempt to balance gender roles in the faculty.

The Lilly Ledbetter Fair Pay Act of 2009

Acting as a companion of sorts to the Equal Pay Act, The Lilly Ledbetter Fair Pay Act primarily addresses the time periods within which pay discrimination claims must be brought. Under this act, the statute of limitations on initiating a claim is "reset" every time an employee is paid in a way that reflects gender discrimination.

For example, if a school purposely paid a female teacher less than a comparably qualified male teacher when she was hired years ago, the statute of limitations is not based on her first paycheck. Rather, the statute starts anew every time she receives a new paycheck. Thus, the school cannot be liable for pay discrimination acts that first occurred in the distant past.

Reviewing and addressing past discriminatory pay practices is a complex matter and should be undertaken only under the direct supervision of the school's employment attorney, to ensure the protection of all concerned.

The Americans with Disabilities Act (ADA) of 1990

Different sections of the ADA may apply to different areas of school operations (e.g., regulations on physical access to buildings for the disabled). Regarding employment, the ADA specifically prohibits an employer from discriminating against individuals with disabilities who are "otherwise qualified" for the position. Employers must make "reasonable accommodations" to remove barriers to employment (such as making the classroom wheelchair-accessible for a disabled faculty candidate or adjusting work schedules for medical needs).

The "accommodation" requirement is balanced by the provision that accommodations need not be unduly burdensome (financially or operationally) on the school. Defining what is "reasonable" or "an undue burden" is often a difficult matter and should always be reviewed with an employment attorney. Schools should note that courts are becoming increasingly skeptical of "undue financial burden" claims as the sole basis for an employer rejecting an accommodation request by a disabled candidate.

All employment applications should include a question that asks, "Are you qualified and able to carry out the duties of this position with or without reasonable accommodations?" (to which the candidate simply answers "yes" or "no"). If the school offers a position to a disabled individual, initiate dialogue about any necessary accommodations after making the job offer. If the employee's recommended solution is not feasible because of cost or operational reasons, seek alternative solutions. Entering into dialogue on accommodations is seen by courts as a matter of good faith, in fulfillment of the ADA's intent. Perhaps no mutually reasonable solution is possible. But this conclusion should only be arrived at after full dialogue with the candidate or employee (and your attorney).

Fair Labor Standards Act (FLSA)

Originally passed in 1938 and updated most recently in 2004, the FLSA defines what positions qualify for overtime pay. For our purposes, faculty positions generally meet the "learned professional" exemption criterion under the law and are deemed "exempt" positions. This means that faculty positions do not qualify for overtime pay under the law.

In compliance with the "exempt" designation, faculty positions must be paid on a "salaried" (rather than "hourly") basis, and deductions generally cannot be made because of the quality or quantity of work. As a practical matter, this means that faculty members must be paid in full for any days on which they perform work. For example, if a teacher goes home sick after teaching for three hours and does not have any more accrued sick time available, he or she must be paid for the full day of work. However, a teacher absent for a full day can then be docked for that day—as no work was performed on that day, assuming that no remaining paid time was available.

Schools should note that some states (California, as one example) have specified additional criteria that teaching positions have to meet to qualify under the exempt status. In addition, schools should be aware that assistant teacher or teacher aide positions do not generally qualify as exempt, and thus must be paid for overtime work.

Consult with your employment attorney to determine the exempt status of any teacher aide or assistant positions in your school. Misclassification (i.e., not paying overtime when required to do so) is a serious matter and can result in fines and penalties.

Fair Credit Reporting Act (FCRA) of 1970

The FCRA impacts schools concerning the background screening process. While the statute's name singles out "credit reports," the FCRA also covers many other types of consumer reports, including background screening reports (e.g., criminal, educational, driving records). If the school orders background reports from an outside vendor as part of its screening process, it must observe the FCRA guidelines. These guidelines are usually easily met.

Before ordering any background reports, the candidate must complete and sign a Background Screening Consent Form. Usually, this completes the school's compliance with FCRA. In cases, however, where a school decides against hiring the candidate due to information contained in the background report (e.g., a past conviction for fraud or harm to children), then it must provide written notification to the candidate.

Written notification includes sending a certified letter to the candidate, with a copy of the background report, indicating the school is considering ending the employment process because of information contained in the candidate's screening report. The candidate has the opportunity to clarify or correct information in the report (usually directly with the report vendor). If correction or clarification does not occur within a reasonable period (usually considered to be five days), then send a second letter officially informing the candidate that you're withdrawing employment consideration.

Review with your background screening vendor the consent form recommended for employers in your state. Certain states also require employers to provide a copy of reports to candidates on request.

Immigration Reform and Control Act (IRCA) of 1986

The IRCA resulted in creating the well-known I-9 form. This form verifies the individual's identity and eligibility to work in the United States. All new employees must complete this form within three days of beginning employment. An employee can meet the law's standards by presenting his or her U.S. passport, driver's license, and Social Security card, or other approved identity and eligibility documents. The school can be subject to fines up to $10,000 per incident for failure to comply with IRCA regulations.

Even though new teachers are typically offered contracts in the spring, do not give them the I-9 form for completion until their first day of work (usually the orientation week in August). This avoids any confusion about their official hire date and the possibility of inadvertently incurring liability for their employment (such as for Worker's Compensation or insurance purposes) before it begins.

Schools may be concerned that they'll have a classroom without a teacher if they don't find out until right before school starts that an employee cannot work because of an I-9 issue (e.g., if a foreign national has not completed the necessary visa paperwork). The employment application should include a question about the candidate's eligibility for employment in the U.S.

Also, the cover letter that accompanies the written contract offer should contain a reference to the identity and eligibility verification form (i.e., I-9 form) the employee must complete at orientation. If the employee cannot provide appropriate proof of identity and eligibility to work in the U.S. within three days of the first day of work, he or she is not permitted to work until the matter is resolved.

COBRA Act of 1986

The Consolidation Omnibus Budget Reconciliation Act (COBRA) refers to the employee's right to continue his or her employee benefits coverage on termination of employment or other "qualifying life events" (e.g., divorce, dependent reaching maximum age). COBRA comes into play when a faculty member resigns or is terminated. In addition, there are other nontermination family circumstances that can trigger COBRA (such as a decrease in employment from full-time to part-time).

On termination or ineligibility for benefits coverage, tell employees of their COBRA rights (which allow them to continue medical and dental coverage at their own expense under the school's policy for up to 18 months). The School Head should ensure the Business Office, Human Resources Department, or other staff members responsible for employee benefits administration observe all COBRA practices. Due to the complex, evolving nature of COBRA rights, the school may consider outsourcing COBRA compliance to a qualified vendor (such as its payroll or insurance provider or other third-party administrator).

While a school has the right to decline to offer COBRA coverage to teachers terminated for gross misconduct (e.g., fraud, embezzlement, fighting), schools should not invoke this right. It often results in an emotionally draining legal battle that detracts from the school's ability to "calm the waters" and attend to faculty culture needs disrupted by any termination of this type.

Keeping it Simple: What an Administrator Really Needs to Know About Employment Law

Except for the more technically oriented regulations (such as FLSA and COBRA), most key employment laws concern employment discrimination. While there are many nuances to each of these laws, a school's primary protection against violating discrimination statutes is simple. A school must take employment actions (e.g., hiring, firing) based solely on job-required skills, experience, and characteristics—and prove that this is what it has done. This is a primary purpose that the Comprehensive Faculty Development Model serves. By establishing hiring, evaluation, termination, and other faculty-related processes that are based on its operating needs and its mission, culture, and values, the school best protects itself from lawsuits, claims, and similar penalties and concerns.

Summary

The school must keep all relevant laws and regulations—and every other step in the Comprehensive Faculty Development Model—in mind throughout its hiring process. Practices outlined in this book are designed to help the school hire, develop, and retain the most qualified, mission-appropriate faculty, and to do so in a legally compliant manner—to avoid lawsuits and, if the school is sued, allow it to prevail in the case.

Faculty Growth Plan Template

Teacher's Name: _____

Date: _____

Goal #1:

_____
_____
_____

Related Characteristics of Professional Excellence (CPE)

_____
_____
_____

Anticipated student outcomes

_____

_____

_____

Steps to achieve this goal

1) _____

2) _____

3) _____

4) _____

5) _____

Resources and support needed to achieve this goal

1) _____

2) _____

3) _____

4) _____

5) _____

Measures of Success/Assessment Tools

1) _____

2) _____

3) _____

4) _____

5) _____

Goal #2:

_____
_____
_____

Related Characteristics of Professional Excellence (CPE)

_____
_____
_____

Anticipated student outcomes

_____
_____
_____

Steps to achieve this goal

1) _____

2) _____

3) _____

4) _____

5) _____

Resources and support needed to achieve this goal

1) _____

2) _____

3) _____

4) _____

5) _____

Measures of Success/Assessment Tools

1) _____

2) _____

3) _____

4) _____

5) _____

Commitment and Accountability

A teacher's commitment to professional growth and renewal, and the administrator's commitment to the success of the teacher, are critical to our students' performance, satisfaction, and enthusiasm, and ultimately to the success of our school and its mission.

With this understanding, we wish jointly to commit and be held accountable for this plan.

Teacher's Signature: _____

Date: _____

Administrator's Signature: _____

Date: _____

Ongoing Reflection – Goal #1

Date	Notes

Ongoing Reflection – Goal #2

Date	Notes

Faculty Evaluation: Sample Review Form

Teacher's Name: _____

Sample Essential Expectations

All faculty members at Exempli Gratia Academy are expected and required to:

1. Overtly support and act in accordance with the school's mission and values.

2. Foster a safe, predictable, and supportive environment for students.

3. Interact with colleagues in a respectful and collegial manner that fosters a healthy faculty culture.

4. Demonstrate appropriate planning and preparation for instruction.

5. Uphold professional standards of personal presentation, punctuality, professional courtesy, and discretion.

6. Appropriately carry out specific assignments including, but not limited to, service learning, advisory programs, assigned supervision, and other areas as determined by the School Head.

7. Maintain professional credentials, as appropriate.

8. Honor the confidentiality of school, student, and family information.

9. Comply with the policies and procedures as articulated in the school's faculty handbook.

10. Authentically engage in self-reflection and annual development of a growth and renewal plan that align with the Characteristics of Professional Excellence (CPE). This includes written goals and progress toward those goals.

❑ Meeting Expectations ❑ Not Meeting Expectations

Notes (for example, if teacher is on a corrective action plan, that would be noted here):

_____

_____

_____

_____

_____

Signed:

(Supervisor) _____

Date _____

Receipt and Review Acknowledged

(Faculty member) _____

Date _____

Sample Correction Action Form

Teacher's Name: _____

Essential Expectation(s) not being met:

_____
_____
_____
_____

Actions required and deadlines:

_____
_____
_____
_____

Meeting/Progress Notes:

Date	Notes	Teacher Initials

Signed:

(Supervisor) _____

Date _____

Receipt and Review Acknowledged

(Faculty member) _____

Date _____

Made in the USA
Columbia, SC
08 May 2021